D0676927

THE FINE ART
OF FRIENDSHIP

1756457

NCMC
BJ
1533
.F8
E53
1985

THE
FINE
ART OF
FRIEND-
SHIP

*Building and Maintaining
Quality Relationships*

Ted W. Engstrom

with Robert C. Larson

Thomas Nelson Publishers
Nashville • Camden • New York

NYACK COLLEGE MANHATTAN

Copyright © 1985 by Ted Engstrom and Robert C. Larson

All rights reserved. Written permission must be secured from the publishers to use or reproduce any part of this book, except for brief quotations in critical reviews or articles.

Published in Nashville, Tennessee, by Thomas Nelson, Inc., and distributed in Canada by Lawson Falle, Ltd., Cambridge, Ontario.

Printed in the United States of America.

Unless otherwise noted, the Scripture quotations in this publication are from the NEW KING JAMES VERSION of the Bible. Copyright © 1979, 1980, 1982, Thomas Nelson Inc., Publishers.

Scripture references marked Phillips are from J. B. Phillips: THE NEW TESTAMENT IN MODERN ENGLISH, revised edition. Copyright © J. B. Phillips 1958, 1960, 1972. Used by permission of Macmillan Publishing Co., Inc.

Scripture reference marked KJV is from the King James Version of the Bible.

Lyrics from "Getting to Know You" on page 39 are from *The King and I*. Copyright © 1951 by Richard Rodgers & Oscar Hammerstein II. Copyright renewed, Williamson Music Co., owner of publication and allied rights throughout the Western Hemisphere and Japan. International copyright secured. All rights reserved. Used by permission.

Excerpt on pages 90–92 is from *Hide or Seek* by James Dobson. Copyright © 1974, 1979 by Fleming H. Revell Company. Published by Fleming H. Revell Company. Used by permission. Also reprinted by permission of Hodder and Stoughton Limited.

Excerpt on pages 71–72 by Harold Wilke is reprinted by permission from *Guideposts* Magazine. Copyright © 1982 by Guideposts Associates, Inc., Carmel, NY 10512.

Excerpt on pages 76–77 is adapted by permission from *Guideposts* Magazine. Copyright © 1984 by Guideposts Associates, Inc., Carmel, NY 10512.

Excerpts on pages 66–68, 86–88, 111–112 by Norman Cousins, Earl Nightingale, and Leo Buscaglia are from *Insight*, a monthly audiocassette series published by Nightingale-Conant Corporation, 7300 North Lehigh Avenue, Chicago, Illinois 60648. All issues are copyright © 1983 by Nightingale-Conant Corporation, and are reprinted by permission.

Excerpt on pages 103–104 are from *Letters to an Unborn Child* by David Ireland with Louis Tharp, Jr. Copyright © 1974 by David E. Ireland and Louis B. Tharp, Jr. Reprinted by permission of Harper and Row, Publishers, Inc.

Excerpts on pages 68–69 are from *Something Beautiful for God* by Malcolm Muggeridge (pages 73–74, 78–79). Copyright © 1971 by The Mother Teresa Committee. Reprinted by permission of Harper and Row, Publishers, Inc.

Excerpt on page 80 is from *Megatrends* © 1982 by John Naisbitt. Published by Warner Books, Inc. Reprinted by permission.

Library of Congress Cataloging in Publication Data

Engstrom, Theodore Wilhelm, 1916-
   The fine art of friendship.
   Bibliography: p.
   1. Friendship.   2. International relations.
I. Larson, Robert C. II. Title.
BJ1533.F8E53   1985   158'.2   85-3065
ISBN 0-8407-5419-1

*Dedicated
to
lovely neighbors
who became
beloved friends*

*Ned and Bette Vessey
and
Herb and Betty Hawkins*

CONTENTS

FOREWORD

I have known Ted Engstrom for nearly forty years. I can tell you that he possesses the rare quality of demonstrating in his own life the truths about which he writes.

Ted Engstrom has learned well the secrets of friendship he advocates. He knows the awesome cost of giving one's self away to a friend. He knows the risks one must take in opening heart and life to another human being. He has tasted the joy of seeing a person whom he befriended blossom into blessed, fruitful living.

Yes, he knows. And you, too, will know the secret of being a friend, if you listen and learn and act upon the principles so clearly presented in these pages.

> Dr. Robert A. Cook
> President
> King's College
> Briarcliff Manor, New York

INTRODUCTION

You do not have to be a special person to make friends. Neither popularity, nor good looks, nor an outgoing personality is required in order to build lasting relationships with others.

The key is whether or not you *want* to be a friend to others. If you do, you can adopt specific attitudes and take certain actions that will make friendship a reality for you. If you want to be a friend, I can help you.

When Thomas Nelson's senior book editor, my friend Peter Gillquist, first approached me about writing a book on making and maintaining friendships, I was both surprised and honored. My first question to Peter was, "Why me?"

Peter revealed that he had attended a very special birthday party my dear friends had sponsored at the Los Angeles Hilton, and he was impressed by the fact that friends of forty years or more had come to celebrate with me—and so honor me by their presence. I've often said that the secret of success is simply to last, and I guess these lasting friendships challenged Peter to believe there might be a helpful

book on the vital theme of making and maintaining friendships.

I didn't take long to agree with Peter and to begin this fascinating project. You will note in this book my inexpressible
appreciation for the way friends have related to me for these
past few decades. These people are my most prized posses-
sions, and in part, this book is my way of telling them so.

The ancient Hebrew writers spoke warmly and frequently
of friendship. What a wonderful thought that King David
of Israel was called "a friend of God." How beautiful was
the friendship between Jonathan and David, between Ruth
and Naomi. Jesus was called the friend of sinners, and He
was criticized for it.

What is a friend? Ask the question to ten different people,
and you'll probably get ten different answers. If we ex-
panded our poll, we might discover as many definitions of
friend as there are friends themselves.

Think for a moment how we use the word *friend*. We say,
"I saw a friend in the supermarket last night," or "Now,
John, he's a *real* friend," or "Honey, let's have a few friends
over for dinner this weekend."

If someone were to press us for our own definition of what
it means to *be a friend* we might make a distinction between
work friends, church friends, close friends, distant friends,
friends we see every day, every year, or at every tenth high
school reunion. But we call them all "friends."

When we focus serious attention on what it really means
to be a friend, certain powerful qualities begin to surface,
such as loyalty, trust, and openness. For extraordinary
friendships, we soon realize that narcissism or any form of
inappropriate self-admiration simply has no place in the relationship. If anything, a preoccupation with self holds

within it the potential of dealing a death blow to the friendship.

The Chinese have a word for it. To the uninitiated, the ancient Chinese language is filled with an overwhelming and baffling array of written characters. Even linguistic experts cannot agree on how many ideographs exist.

On a recent trip to Hong Kong, I decided to do something about my gross lack of knowledge about a language now spoken by almost one-fourth of our world's people. I spent an evening with a close friend who is also a scholar of the Chinese language. In two hours, he took me on a breathtaking, whirlwind oral tour of China and its more than five thousand years of history. During the course of our visit, we discussed the Chinese word for "friend."

The current, everyday word for "friend" in China today is *peng yu,* but its history goes back many centuries. My tutor drew a primitive Chinese character that represented the magnificent tail of a bird called "Phoenix." This bird was so marvelous in every detail that the written character came to mean something much more than "Phoenix." It slowly developed into a more generic meaning of "completeness...the sum total of physical beauty."

My friend proceeded to tell me that throughout the ensuing years, the literal meaning of the word was completely lost while the written character took on today's meaning of "friend, friendship, or close association."

"Why was that?" I asked.

Outer, visible beauty arrests our attention to be sure, but the true, inner beauties in people—the elegance, truth, and consistency that live within the soul of a friend—are irresistible. In friendships, hearts relate to each other. Like the flock of birds that followed the ancient Phoenix into the heavens, people will do just about anything to follow a man or a woman who has developed a friendly heart.

In this book my aim has been to help readers realize how precious friendship is. It cannot be purchased, borrowed, or manufactured. It must be cultivated as a tender plant.

I cannot claim that I am a special friend. I do know I cherish the countless friends that are mine without merit. I am simply passing on the principles governing human friendship I have learned over more years than I care to discuss! I hope you can and will use these principles in your life to recognize the value of friendship, to become a friend to others, and to accept the friendship offered to you.

This book could not have come into print without the dedicated research, loving assistance, and skill of my dear friend Robert C. Larson. He has worked with me as a colleague for many years, but far more importantly, he has been—and is—my friend. To him I owe the deepest gratitude.

This, then, is the subject of these pages: friendship. I offer ten powerful—and often overlooked—principles to help you develop the skills, sensitivities, and qualities that are essential in learning the fine art of friendship.

Ted W. Engstrom

It is only by risking our persons from one hour to the next that we live at all.
—*William James*

1

THOSE "IMPOSSIBLE" CASES

I wasn't particularly fond of Don, and many fellow students didn't like him. He was anything but a scholar, and his teachers were unanimous in their speculation that he probably wouldn't amount to much.

Meanwhile, I had a problem. I was in charge of the public relations department at Taylor University in central Indiana, and I needed someone to help me type news releases and feature stories for the school paper, the *Marion Chronicle,* and other local papers.

Don, for all his inabilities in general, happened to be the fastest typist around. Although I did it against my better instincts, I gave him a job. What I didn't realize at the time was that he was also the most inaccurate typist on campus! When all was said and done, Don really didn't seem to have much going for him that would be helpful to us in the office. Still, there was a chemistry between us that I wouldn't fully understand until much later.

His typing didn't improve much in the weeks and months he worked for me, but he slowly began to make his mark in university athletics. He started breaking school baseball records one after another, and he still holds the crown for the highest consistent batting average for any four-year player. Most important of all, as a freshman he made a firm commitment to Jesus Christ as his Savior and Lord.

To make a long story short, Don Odle remained at Taylor after his graduation to become the winningest basketball coach in the school's history, and at his retirement the fifth winningest coach in the United States. For thirty-five years he coached there and modeled discipline, courage, patience, and an inner peace that helped shape the lives of literally hundreds of young men.

He went on to become the founder of Venture for Victory, an international basketball team of Christians that has carried the good news of God's love to villages, cities, barrios, and prisons all over the world. In the process, literally hundreds of thousands of people have said yes to a relationship with Jesus Christ.

Don later became assistant to the president of Taylor University, and in that position he was able to touch other lives that have gone on to ministries that circle the globe.

Don Odle—the fast typist who couldn't spell. The poor student. The kid with little potential. For some reason, I had chosen to be his friend—and he had chosen to be mine. Over the years he has become one of the best friends I've ever had. He's not just my friend; he is a friend to the world! Our years together have taught me a powerful principle of friendship essential to building a lasting relationship:

---

1.   **We must decide to develop friendships in which we demand nothing in return.**

Love, in order to work, must be unconditional. Just as God accepts us on an "as is" basis, so too must we enter into friendships based on taking the other person unconditionally into the relationship.

I think a lot about those early days with Don, and I try to remember to keep the same attitude toward all the "Dons" that come my way every day. As much as I like to believe I can spot a diamond in the rough, I still don't always manage to do it. Like the day I received a long distance telephone call.

I was busy and didn't want to be disturbed. I was told it was urgent so I reluctantly picked up the phone. A young man's voice said, "Dr. Engstrom, I have decided I would like to work with World Vision."

Since he had me on the line, I figured I might as well give him sixty seconds, and then I'd be through with him. I found it wasn't that easy. He wanted to see me personally. I said I was on my way to New York City. He said, "I'll meet you there."

We had dinner in New York. I didn't really respond to him warmly. He was young and brash. I told him he probably wouldn't fit in, but he would not take no for an answer!

I said, "Well, what do you like to do?"

He replied, "I like to solve problems."

With that he had my attention. I started to listen more carefully. Solve problems, eh? I admitted we certainly had problems.

He asked, "When do I start?"

Now he had me. I told him I'd give him $1000 (for one month) to help us solve some problems. Do you know what? In the months and years to follow he not only solved one *problem* after another, but he also designed and put into motion the tremendously successful World Vision Love Loaf program that has already raised more than $15 million to feed hungry, destitute people throughout the world.

His name is Bobb (he even spells his first name funny) Biehl. Today, he is a dear, cherished friend.

It's true. Friendships often demand from us wild, even unreasonable risks. Sometimes they turn out to be the best, most exciting, most productive relationships of all. Try making a friend of someone you may not be overly impressed with at first. Who knows? He may set some records or help you raise $15 million. In the process, he or she may become a cherished friend. You'll never know unless you try.

The Acid Test of Friendship

Have you ever felt "ripped off" in a friendship, been conned into a relationship that never was really there in the first place? How do you tell a true friend from a pseudofriend?

"It's not very difficult," says Eugene Kennedy, professor of psychology at Loyola University of Chicago. He continues:

> The tests that have been applied to friendships throughout the ages apply very well today. If you find, for example, that there are people you can't be with unless you're doing something together—skiing, playing handball, going to a play; in other words, a third thing to which you both direct your attention—then that person may not be as good a friend as you think.... The real test of friendship is: Can you literally do nothing with the other person? Can you enjoy together those moments of life that are utterly simple? They are the moments that people look back on at the end of life

and number as the most sacred experiences they've ever had.[1]

Think back in your life, and you'll probably agree the professor is right. The truly great moments of friendships have been when you were really doing nothing in particular with your friend, when you were making no demands whatsoever on the relationship. Yet, for some people, this "doing nothing" is a terrifying experience.

In a healthy, nurturing friendship, the risk of doing nothing is seldom a threat. For example, you lie in a sun-drenched meadow of wild flowers at eleven thousand feet after an all-morning mountain climb. The elevation has your heart pumping as it has never pumped before. You are so exhausted you literally have nothing to say. You are with your friend, and that is enough.

Or the phone rings at two in the morning. It is your friend telling you his teen-age son has just been involved in a terrible automobile accident. Through his tears he tells you his boy is not expected to live. With a lump rising in your throat, you race to the emergency room just to be there, not to say, or necessarily *do* anything. Just to be there with your friend. And just being there is enough. Haven't you known this feeling?

More and more this is how my wife, Dorothy, and I feel about our adult children. We experience a simple, quiet joy and relaxation in just being together.

How to Find Friends Tailor-made for No Demands

In many ways, finding a true friend is much like finding happiness or riches or great fame. Real joy—the kind that lives in the marrow of our bones—seldom comes to us when we spend all our time trying to achieve it. Instead, it's almost always a side benefit to being totally immersed in some fulfilling piece of work. In similar fashion, great wealth historically has not necessarily come to those who set their minds on riches alone. Fame, too, has often been no more than the by-product of the great dedication and work of an ordinary person who chose to do great things.

It's the same with friendship. More than anything else, it seems to be little more than a spin-off of who we are and what we feel and believe about ourselves. In fact, the most important element in building a friendship seems to be the ability to accept ourselves as we are and then to *be* that person so that others perceive us as genuine. I think we'll all discover in the process those friends who are tailor-made for us. Take this story for example.

In March of 1983, UPI released a story about a five-year-old leukemia victim. The emotion of the scenario tore at the heartstrings of the entire nation. It was all about a very special friendship, one that clearly illustrates principle number one in being a friend—that of not demanding anything in return.

About one month after his parents learned their son, "P. J." Dragan, had leukemia, the child began receiving a variety of get well messages. He received gifts, cleverly written letters, poems, and drawings. The presents all came from an unnamed party called "Magic Dragon." The special trademark of Magic Dragon's gifts was a big green bow.

As the weeks and months wore on, little P. J.'s treatments grew long and painful. But there was one consolation. Magic Dragon's surprises arrived at the house with clockwork regularity. P. J.'s favorite gift was a stuffed dragon—a friend that became more realistic to the boy as the disease progressed.

P. J.'s father was a Detroit policeman. At one point, he tried to track down Magic Dragon's hidden identity. However, he changed his mind when he discovered the trouble to which Magic Dragon had gone in order to cover his or her tracks.

When little P. J. went into the hospital, the prized toy dragon received the same treatment the boy did. When a bandage was put on P. J., the dragon got one too. That little stuffed toy with the big green bow pulled P. J. through some of the most difficult times of his illness.

Unfortunately, five-year-old P. J. lost his battle, and shortly after listening to his favorite record, "Puff the Magic Dragon," the brave little boy died. Hundreds of friends and relatives paid their final respects to P. J. and contributed to the vast array of flowers that occupied most of the room where his little body lay. As you would have expected, in the middle of the display was a gigantic bouquet of daisies tied affectionately together with a big green bow.[2]

"Magic Dragon," if you're reading this book, I want to say thank you from all of us whose lives are a lot different because of what you did. You made no demands on P. J., and you chose anonymity to do what you were moved to do.

But more than that you have shown us all that finding a tailor-made friend is basically little more than finding people in need and then helping them all we can. You didn't mind risking it with P. J. I hope we won't either. Thank you, Magic Dragon.

But I've Been Hurt Before...

How many times have you heard someone say that? I loved once, and it didn't work out, so I'll never love again. I was once his friend, but he turned on me. I'll never trust again.

It reminds me of the line from the great American literary figure, H. L. Mencken, who said, "There's always an easy solution to every human problem—neat, plausible, and wrong." Nothing could be more unfortunate than to act like the proverbial cat who sat on one hot stove and vowed never to sit on any stove again. Yet it happens all the time. Every day, hurt and disappointment keep hundreds of thousands of people from enjoying the fantastic rewards that come from friendships.

What can we do? Perhaps the language of motivation literature may move us along. We have phrases like, "When the going gets tough, the tough get going," or in Robert Schuller's words, "Tough times never last, but tough people do," "profit from your problems," and "harness your handicaps."

You might respond that life is hard and you have been hurt often. That may be true, but that is true for all of us. When a friend has hurt or disappointed us, it's often difficult for us to bounce back. That's when Henry Ford's encouraging words can help us. The famous car maker once said: "Failure is only the opportunity to begin again, more intelligently." Perhaps we were somewhat naive in the friendship, or we didn't really know what was expected of us. Maybe we expected more of our friend than he or she was able to give. These are all realistic possibilities.

Will you take some risks to receive the rewards of friendship by setting some enormous goals for yourself, or will you settle for less than the best? Let's face it, just about everything seems impossible at first. Even that greatest salesman of them all, J. C. Penney admitted that when he said, "The hardest thing of all is just getting started! The first sale is always the hardest."

If you will begin, if you will consider going out on a limb in a friendship with no demands on your friend, you will discover a treasure no amount of money could buy. But it will seldom come easy.

In fact, the greatest lie of all is that friendship will come automatically to us free and clear, without our risking anything or doing something to pursue it. The song says, "It Ain't Necessarily So." Better than that, it's not so at all!

A healthy, nurturing friendship demands work. True friendship is never a one-way street. If it is, it won't be one for long. Instead, friendship is a dynamic, ever-moving force that involves the commitment, energy, discipline, and caring of two people. The Scriptures ask us, "Can two walk together, unless they are agreed?" (Amos 3:3). The implied answer is, "Of course not!" Two people must speak the same language to communicate, and friends must determine to speak the language of friendship.

A good friend doesn't say, "Take care of me. Pay me my due." A person who seeks a meaningful friendship doesn't exploit a friend. In friendship there is a yielding to the other, with the full knowledge the golden rule is as applicable today as the day it was first given to the children of Israel: Do unto others as you would have them do unto you.

In the process, we need to remember that a friendship is not a right; it is a privilege. Friendships will survive only if we give them the careful attention and nurture they must have. Long-term happy relationships indicate a person has a strong sense of self-worth and the capacity to give himself or herself without fear of being depleted.

Will you often need to go out on a limb? Yes, your friendships may involve tremendous risks—risks of giving and not necessarily receiving or of putting yourself on the line without being assured a payoff.

There are no thirty-day or thirty-year guarantees with friendship. As you stretch your caring, and as before God you expand your compassion, you will discover the truth of the words of the nineteenth-century author George Eliot who wrote that friendship is the "inexpressible comfort of feeling safe with a person, having neither to weigh thoughts nor measure words."

I've put the principle of *demanding nothing in return* first on my list for a reason. Maybe you've tried too hard to be friends with people who for some reason had no need for your friendship. This time, try for a friend that nobody else may want.

Are you ready, willing, and able to take the plunge into what may be the most wonderful experience of your life? Are you ready to reach out to that someone and begin a relationship with no strings attached? Perhaps there is a "P. J. Dragon" ready to receive the love only you can give. All it takes to get started is open eyes, an open heart, and the open willingness to be a friend.

Together we stick; divided we're stuck.
—*Evon Hedley*

2

FRIENDSHIP
—A PIECE OF CAKE?

In chapter one, we saw that we need to develop friendships in which we demand nothing in return. If we are out solely for our own interests, an authentic friendship with another will be impossible. Principle number two is another important brick in our "friendship house."

It was the day before Thanksgiving. My wife, Dorothy, was doing some last minute shopping. She had a short list: one jar of cranberries.

She parked the car, walked into the store, and marched directly to the shelf where she knew the cranberries would be displayed. To her surprise there was only one jar left, but one jar was all she needed.

Her hand went out to remove the lone jar from the shelf when she saw five other fingers grasp the same jar. It was another woman who also needed only one additional item to complete the things she needed for her Thanksgiving feast. That item? Cranberries.

In the spirit of the season, each insisted the other take the jar. Finally, the manager of the store intervened and said there were more cranberries in the back room. An innocent encounter with another shopper? Not really, because that is only the beginning of the story.

Dorothy proceeded to give her new friend, Bette, one of her favorite recipes for a pink and fluffy cranberry sherbet. After the holidays, the two women got together. Before long, even Bette's husband, Ned, would stop by the house just to talk.

During one of Ned's stopovers, he told Dorothy, "You know, like you, we've just moved to this area. I wonder if you'd help Bette get out and meet some new people. It would mean a great deal to me—and to both of us." Dorothy was delighted to be able to spend more time with Bette.

Dorothy invited Bette to join her at a fellowship group of Christian women in the neighborhood, for a time of neighborly friendship and Bible study. It was apparently just what Bette needed, because that one meeting made an indelible impression on her life.

Dorothy and Bette went back to our house afterward for coffee. That was when Dorothy started stalling. There was also to be a prayer meeting that afternoon, but Dorothy reasoned it would be a bit much to invite Bette to that too. It would just be too much gospel in one day.

Then Dorothy said, "Oh, come on. Why don't you join me for the entire afternoon?" It was surely the prompting of the Holy Spirit for Dorothy to extend that invitation, because at the close of that afternoon prayer meeting, Bette quietly slipped to her knees and, brushing back the tears that ran down her cheeks, asked Jesus Christ to take over her life.

That was more than twenty years ago. Today, Bette, Ned, and their five beautiful children have become some of our dearest friends. More important than that, each member of the Vessey family has invited that best friend of all into their hearts—Jesus Christ.

It all started when two women reached for a lone jar of cranberries. I love to tell that story, because it proves that friendships can begin just about anywhere. Even in a busy supermarket the day before Thanksgiving.

How about you? Are you willing to step forward and be a friend to someone who doesn't have one? Your new friendships can be launched with a simple smile, perhaps with just a handshake after a business or civic meeting. Friendships can be started in a classroom, at a church outing, on the tennis court, or in a doctor's waiting room. Often mutual pain or suffering—the really tough, hard times—brings people together. However, it happens, people do become friends. Often special friends. At the same time, lapses of caring can be devastating.

During a memorable day in Sweden some years ago, my actions dealt a severe blow to my reputation. My good friend Jack Sonneveldt and I were traveling throughout Sweden on some speaking engagements. We had been graciously entertained and felt most welcome in that great country of my forefathers.

One day, however, we simply had a need to be on our own. We didn't want any guides, tours, cathedrals, or zoos. But guess what? We got them all. Our host in Stockholm insisted a kind gentleman be our guide and chauffeur one sleepy Swedish Sunday afternoon.

There was no way we could get out of this prearranged tour. Jack and I shrugged our shoulders, lethargically got into Sven's car, and began the tour. It was hot that day in Stockholm, which only made matters worse. During our four-hour journey throughout the city, I'm convinced we saw every park, every tree, every church, and every animal in the Stockholm zoo. To add to the boredom, Sven said absolutely nothing. Perhaps twice he grunted something in broken English; we knew he had no command of the language.

Jack and I started talking to each other. No response from Sven. We complained a bit more. Sven said nothing. Finally, I turned to Jack and said in a voice I now wish had not been so loud, "Man, how are we going to get rid of this *cimice* (pronounced "chimiche")?" Suddenly Sven jerked his head around and gave me one of those looks I hope I never see again. I blustered something apologetically in English, only to feel the car make a sharp right turn in the direction of our hotel.

Jack and I sat there in stunned silence. Sven brought the car to a screeching halt in front of the hotel, and Jack and I got out. I extended my hand to Sven in thanks. The handshake he returned was the likes of a cold, limp Swedish sardine. Sven couldn't wait to get out of there.

Neither could I.

Later I asked our host if Sven could speak English. "Oh, yes," said our friend, "he's just rather shy. In fact, he speaks several languages fluently." I asked if Sven could speak Italian. "Oh, sure," said the host. "In fact, he travels regularly to Italy on business."

By now my face was ashen. My heart was stone gray too. In utter frustration and fatigue and in a voice loud and clear, I had insulted our gracious driver. Little did I know Sven would recognize *cimice* as the Italian word for "bedbug"! I hadn't meant to offend him, but I had. I had some terribly important explaining to do. For those few moments that Sunday afternoon I had made a terrible assumption, and in the process had forgotten principle number two for being a friend.

2. It takes a conscious effort to nurture an authentic interest in others.

I'm happy to say I feel I learned my lesson that hot, sultry, summer day in Stockholm, a lesson I hope I'll never forget. It was an embarrassing but nonetheless important turning point in showing me how I viewed people. I really wasn't the caring person I thought I was. I wasn't all that interested in others who weren't doing something I wanted. I had offended Sven terribly, and if he ever reads this book I want him to know that I have an apology for him that is now thirty years overdue. I will also tell him I've never called anyone a *cimice* since! If anything, that experience in Stockholm made me almost hypersensitive to the needs of others, particularly in a strange, unfamiliar environment.

I have had many experiences that have showed me how important it is to make a conscious effort to show sincere interest in someone else. One such occurrence happened in Calcutta, India.

Most international flights arrive in this legendary Indian city late at night or early dawn. As the pastor of Carey Memorial Church, my friend Walter Corlett, drove me to the Great Eastern Hotel, I once again looked out into the darkness at the mass of suffering humanity that makes Calcutta one of the most heart-breaking cities in the world.

It was almost 2:00 A.M. I was exhausted from the long transoceanic flight and could think only of the few hours of sleep I would get before a busy schedule that would begin in less than six hours. When I arrived at the door of the hotel, a teen-age boy grabbed my trouser leg and pleaded, "Shoe-shine, mister? I give you good shoeshine."

Shoeshine! "You've got to be kidding," I said, looking at my watch. I said I was tired, but perhaps tomorrow. Well, tomorrow was only six hours away, and when I made my way out of the hotel those few hours later, the shoeshine boy was there again.

"Shoeshine, mister?"

"OK," I said, "but I want a good one."

"I give you best shoeshine in Calcutta," he said.

And he did. But he also gave me something else. During the next several days, that young boy gave me the opportunity to become his friend.

His name was Dwarka Das. He was fifteen years old, a Hindu, and he had recently been married. Every month he would send virtually all his earnings to his wife and parents who lived in the sacred city of Benares. He could get no work in Benares, so he had come for employment in Calcutta. During the next five days Dwarka Das and I talked regularly over his shoeshine box. I've never had so many shoeshines in one week. (And he really did give me the best shine I've ever had!)

Dwarka Das would tell me about his faith in the ancient beliefs of Hinduism and its many gods. I would then speak of my love for Jesus Christ.

One day as I was leaving the hotel, Dwarka Das gave me a photo of himself, signed "from your friend in Calcutta." I later gave him a Polaroid picture of me. For months we corresponded with each other, he with the help of a friend at the Carey Baptist Church.

Eighteen months later I once again found myself in Calcutta. Somehow Dwarka Das learned of my arrival and arranged for flowers to be placed in my room. Once again I treated myself to more shoeshines than my shoes needed. By then our friendship was blossoming. We had both taken a genuine interest in each other—a young, newly married shoeshine boy and a middle-aged executive with a large Christian organization. But there were really no differences when it came to being a friend.

During the months that followed, I sent Dwarka Das books, letters, and photographs. I also asked Christian friends in Calcutta to give him a Bible in his own language.

One day I received a long letter from my young friend in which he told me he had decided to become a follower of Jesus. The letter went on talking about all our meetings together and how much he valued our friendship. The final sentence in the last letter I received is one I'll never forget. He wrote, "Mr. Ted, you give me many things. Books, letters, good tips for shoeshine. But one thing most good you give me is you are my friend. Thank you, Mr. Ted, for you be my friend."

Thank you, too, Dwarka Das, for being mine and for reminding me that the honest-to-goodness interest we have in each other is the stuff real friendships are made of. But it takes a singleness of purpose and a strong commitment to make it happen.

Earl Nightingale in his helpful and practical audiocassette series, *Insight*, tells a fascinating story of the American team of mountain climbers who conquered Mount Everest. I've paraphrased his account here.

It seems that before the team of climbers left the United States, each of the skilled mountaineers was questioned at length by a psychiatrist. During the session the doctor asked each of them this question: "Will you get to the top of Everest?"

The interviewer received a wide assortment of responses.

Some said, "Well, doctor, I'm going to do my best," or "I'm sure going to try," or "I'm going to work at it." Of course every climber knew of Everest's formidable reputation and its almost impossible peak. But one of the men, a slightly built person, had a totally different answer. When the psychiatrist asked him the question, he thought for a moment and then quietly answered, "Yes, I will." Not surprisingly, he was the first one who made it to the peak of Mount Everest.

Yes, I will—three of the most potent words in our language. Whether spoken quietly, loudly, or silently, those three words have propelled more people to success and have been responsible for more human achievement than all other words in the English language combined.

They are also good words for people who feel they don't have the built-in desire to make friends. Let me say this to you. Right now, you can make a conscious choice to develop genuine, authentic friendships with people you would not naturally seek out—friendships that can begin by your affirming those three words that put a slightly built climber on the top of Mount Everest: *Yes, I will!*

Nothing in the world can take the place of that kind of persistence. The possibilities for personal joy and fulfillment are endless when you take the initiative and decide to be a friend.

Have you ever read Zane Grey's books that chronicle the life and times of both heroes and ne'er-do-wells in the Wild West? If you have you'll remember that the books invariably open with the scene of a tall, lean stranger who saunters into town. His eyes are usually a cool, steel gray, his jaw is firmly set, and his body is covered with the alkali residue borne of days and weeks in the saddle. As he pushes his way through the swinging doors of the two-story town saloon, everyone in the room is well aware his weathered hands are never far from the two gleaming six-shooters strapped to his thighs.

This stranger has no friends or acquaintances and seems perfectly content to keep it that way. This stereotyped cowpoke is the epitome of the loner. He is portrayed as an individual who has no one and *needs* no one.

Such people make good characters for interesting stories of the Old West, but in real life it's an unrealistically lonely way to live. Who wants to live as a law unto himself or herself with absolutely no concern for others? You probably don't live on the open plains like Grey's lonely cowboy, but you may know all about the personal pain of isolation and loneliness. How can you start to make contact with others? What do you do to get out of your well-formed rut, which is really nothing more than a grave with the ends knocked out of it? Well, consider this:

1. *Work at being a helpful, considerate person.* Regardless of your age, sex, physical ability, or I.Q., you can be helpful, considerate, and kind to those around you. It might be no more than helping a neighbor work on his or her car. Perhaps your school or church needs volunteers for a special project. If you're a grandmother or grandfather, you may want to make yourself available at a day care center a few hours each week to read and tell stories to children who have no grandparents. The ways in which you can be helpful— break out of your isolation cycle—are endless. In the process, you will also discover you are learning how to be a friend.

Yet at the same time you will want to be careful not to make yourself a nuisance to people who are perhaps not ready for your help. I like the J. B. Phillips paraphrase of

1 Corinthians 13, which reads, in part,

> [Love] is not possessive: it is neither anxious to impress nor
> does it cherish inflated ideas of its own importance. Love
> has good manners and does not pursue selfish advantage. It
> is not touchy....Love knows no limit to its endurance, no
> end to its trust, no fading of its hope.

This marvelous treatise on love continues to explore the
full-ranged magnitude of what a love based on a relationship
with Jesus Christ can do to a person's life. Such a love cannot exist when turned inward. When this happens, it becomes narcissism, a greedy form of self-love, and the church
fathers, almost with one voice, called self-love "the mother
of all sins." When we seek the best in and for others, and
when we give their interests priority, we soon discover there
is absolutely no reason in the world to be like that lonely
stranger in Grey's Western novels who loved only himself
and perhaps his horse. In the process of our "new thinking," we move one step closer to learning the fine art of
friendship.

2. *Start believing in people.* Undoubtedly you can come up
with literally thousands of reasons why you *shouldn't* believe
in people. After all, you've been disappointed, hurt, frustrated, put down, turned down, and let down—just like I
have. That always hurts, does it not? I am reminded of the
sad-sack businessman who had a reason every single month
why business was bad. His list of people-problems bears repeating:

> January—People spent all their cash for the holidays.
> February—All the best customers have gone South.
> March—Unseasonably cold and too rainy.

April—Everybody is preoccupied with income taxes.
May—Too much rain, farmers distressed.
June—Too little rain, farmers distressed.
July—Heat has everyone down.
August—Everybody away on vacation.
September—Everybody is back, broke.
October—Customers waiting to see how fall clearance sales turn out.
November—People upset over election results.
December—Customers need money for the holidays.

Frankly, I wonder how he could stay in business long enough to put his analysis into printed form!

Look what happens to you—yes, to you—when you adopt the reverse attitude that says, "Today, it's going to be different. Today, I'm going to start believing in people! I'm going to take a chance on trusting." When you do, stand back, because the results are going to be earthshattering.

In fact, think with me for a moment of a creative alternative to solve our business friend's problems. What about something like this:

January—Post-holiday sales—free 30-day credit
February—Florida vacation specials
March—End-of-the-season sale on energy-efficient space heaters
April—Free income tax guide with $20 purchase
May—50 percent off special shipment of umbrellas
June—Free seminar: Ten Secrets to More Efficient Farming
July—Sale on air conditioners and floor fans
August—25 percent off on camping equipment and free road maps
September—Back-to-school sales; drawings for football tickets

October—Pre-fall clearance specials
November—Rollback of prices to Election Day four years
  ago
December—Holiday sale; no payments until March 1

The difference is attitude! You've heard the lines of poetry that read, "Two men looked out from prison bars; one saw mud, the other stars." It can be the same for you, and it can begin right now.

It's amazing, isn't it, that we feel some people have a so-called "Midas touch"? Upon closer investigation we discover their positive, never-take-no-for-an-answer attitude was far superior to that of anyone within miles, and it helped them accomplish their goals. *Attitude* is the magical word. Salesmen know it. Politicians know it. People who get ahead in life know that attitude is their secret weapon.

When you eliminate domination by the negative and believe in those around you, you are going to make some amazing discoveries. You'll find out that folks aren't as bad as you thought. Before long, you'll be echoing the words of that great, gifted humanitarian, Albert Schweitzer, who said,

> It is not enough merely to exist. It's not enough to say, "I'm earning enough to live and to support my family. I do my work well. I'm a good father. I'm a good husband. I'm a good churchgoer." That's all very well. But you must do something more. Seek always to do some good, somewhere. Every man has to seek in his own way to make his own self more noble and to realize his own true worth. You must give some time to your fellowman.[1]

How do you start believing in people? Start at home. Instead of telling your sons or daughters how poorly they are doing in school or scolding them for forgetting to take out the trash, do something to gain their affection. Give them a hug, and tell them you are proud of them. Find something you can honestly say you like about them. Say it with enthusiasm. Don't nag. Encourage. Do the same thing with your neighbors, preacher, fellow employees, and spouse. The list of people to believe in is endless. You'll not only start feeling better about your own ability to maintain relationships at virtually every level, but you'll also discover that developing a real interest in people is your amazing secret in learning the fine art of friendship.

3. *Keep the lines of communication open with people you care about.* It's almost a cliche to say we need open communication in marriage or any intimate relationship, but still, I don't think we can say it enough. Judson Swihart writes,

> Some people are like medieval castles. Their high walls keep them safe from being hurt. They protect themselves emotionally by permitting no exchange of feelings with others. No one can enter. They are secure from attack. However, inspection of the occupant finds him or her lonely, rattling around his castle alone. The castle dweller is a self-made prisoner. He or she needs to feel loved by someone, but the walls are so high that it is difficult to reach out or for anyone else to reach in.[2]

It is impossible to be a friend when you spend your time building walls. I know something of this from painful personal experience, because for too many years I took what I thought was legitimate cover under my "stubborn Nordic personality" or "work schedule" or "travel plans" or "the Lord's work." You name it. Often what I was really doing was building high, unfriendly walls of rejection, of exclusion, and of judgment. I know I still have a long way to go before I will have removed completely some of the remaining barriers, but I'm thankful to a gracious God that I'm making progress.

Easy? No. One day at a time, one step at a time, we must begin to dismantle those frightening fortresses of isolation and loneliness one brick at a time—starting now. Make that one long overdue phone call to a loved one. You may have to swallow some of your pride, but it won't be all that difficult. Once you decide to make the effort to develop an authentic interest in others, you will have tapped one of the most powerful sources available in learning to become a friend.

Man is more interesting than men.
God made him and not them in His image.
Each one is more precious than all.
—Andre Gide

3

RECOGNIZING INDIVIDUALITY

In Rodgers and Hammerstein's delightful musical *The King and I,* Anna, the English schoolteacher, arrives at the palace of the king of Siam. Her job is to tutor the king's many children—an assignment that is at best difficult, at worst almost impossible. Everything for Anna is difficult: the Siamese culture, the time-worn traditions, and the inferior role of women. She also has to deal with a most uncooperative king.

Before long, however, Anna and the king's children develop friendship and mutual admiration that could well be models for anyone who ever plans to work in a foreign land. Misunderstandings are quietly reduced to a minimum. The children, isolated in their palace fairyland, slowly learn of the big world outside.

Then one day Anna gathers her young charges around her and expresses her growing affection to the children in song.

> Getting to know you, getting to feel free and easy,
> Getting to like you, getting to hope you like me.
> Haven't you noticed, suddenly I'm bright and breezy
> Because of all the beautiful and new
> Things I'm learning about you day by day.[1]

Anna made a tremendous discovery. She found that the more she got to know the children, the more she was able to see them as wonderful, beautiful human beings. Every day she learned something new and special about them, and the fresh discoveries made her glad to be alive. She quickly realized it would take time to learn all she still had to know.

Enter the king. To him, everything about Anna was strange. Why did she make such outrageous demands of him, such as wanting her own house outside the palace? Why did Anna not realize her head was never to be raised higher than the king's? In fact the monarch had so many problems with Anna that after a while instead of listing his grievances, he would simply grumble: "Etcetera, etcetera, etcetera." To him, Anna was the definition of a "puzzlement"!

Enter you and I. Whether we travel to distant, unfamiliar places to work or play, or whether we stay at home, there is much about our relationships that is little short of a puzzlement.

Celebrate Our Differences

Just as no two snowflakes or fingerprints are alike, so are we all different in size, shape, color, temperament, interests, convictions, and lifestyle. We are different in every conceivable aspect. Yet, in spite of these contrasts, we still permit differences to remain insurmountable barriers to what could be wonderful friendships. We hold opposing political views that compel us to shout at one another. We are suddenly hurt, offended, or misunderstood by someone, perhaps even by a friend, and before we know it, we hesitate to trust again.

Many years ago I had great difficulty in accepting people who for whatever reason had gone through the pain of divorce. I was able to marshal any number of reasons why the breakup of a marriage was a disqualifier for a deepening friendship.

As I look back, I see I was rigid, not righteous. I was more concerned with the letter of the law than I was with loving the divorced people so desperately in need of friends. Such a posture prevented my becoming the friend I sincerely wanted to be.

One day, I realized I was the one who was losing out. What I needed to do was not to stop hating divorce but to start loving divorced individuals. I was the one who needed to break free, to begin accepting and loving and forgiving.

While I continue to this day to hold marriage to be an inviolate, sacred trust, I realize I lived my life with a clouded vision of what Paul meant when he said, "Let all bitterness, wrath, anger, clamor, and evil speaking be put away from you, with all malice. And be kind to one another, tenderhearted, forgiving one another, just as God in Christ also forgave you" (Eph. 4:31–32).

The breakthrough for me came when I started to make even the smallest effort to get to know and love people who had experienced the pain of divorce. (Remember, friendship principle number two talked about developing an authentic interest in others.) I can still remember the time and the place when I got on my knees to ask God for grace and wisdom, not to promote the tragedy of divorce, but to pursue the joy of friendship. What is the principle involved here?

**3. Each of us is a one-of-a-kind creation. Therefore,
it will always take time—often a long time—to
understand one another.**

This story helps me understand some of that.

After the death of their religious leader, a large group of
his most faithful disciples came together and talked about
the things their great mentor had taught them. When it was
Rabbi Schneur Zalman's turn, he asked them: "Do you
know why our master went to the pond every day at dawn
and stayed there for a little while before coming home
again?" They did not know why. Rabbi Zalman continued:
"He was learning the song with which the frogs praise God.
It takes a very long time to learn that song." [2]

You and I must learn it takes a long time to learn the special song that comes from the heart of a friend. When the
music finally begins, that friendship will become a sym-
phony of delight, but it will always take time—and often
longer than we would like.

During the period after Bob Pierce's departure as president of World Vision, I was often approached to assume the
leadership of the organization. But I knew it would not be
right. While Bob Pierce and I had begun to mend our differences, I felt it would have been an awkward position for
me to fill. I determined never to seek the presidency of
World Vision.

I knew a man I considered to be just the right person for
the job. He was well known in the world of Christian leadership, he had exceptional communications skills, and he

was committed to the kind of ministry World Vision was doing around the globe. His name was W. Stanley Mooneyham. He came to my office, and we talked.

I told him I thought he would make a strong president, and he proved me right. It was the beginning of one of the most satisfying friendships I've ever had. For the next dozen years, Stan and I made a mutual commitment to get to know one another.

For Stan, the first year was one of learning the ropes, but he was a fast learner. After those first twelve months, he was off and running. Since both of us spent more than half our time away from each other in travel and meetings, we made it a point to spend uninterrupted time together when we were in the office. There, we had an open door policy. We promised each other neither of us would ever be too busy to talk. There was absolute freedom between us to discuss anything.

In the good years that followed, we attended international conferences together, we participated in seminars both at home and abroad, we had breakfasts and lunches together, and we even became neighbors. People who knew us both well often remarked, "But you two are so totally different!" And it's true. Our styles of leadership were and are different, but we always assumed those differences would be our greatest strengths.

We also predetermined not to let those differences get in the way of our friendship. We recognized our individuality and made a strong effort to take whatever time was necessary to get to know one another. I'm convinced the success of our long personal and professional relationship has been due in large measure to just that. We accepted the fact we were different, and we determined to celebrate it. Stan and I didn't just become friends. We worked at our friendship over time. Our friendship was intentional. Those same "intentional" relationships can also work for you.

It's a time-worn cliché but as true today as the day it was first spoken: If you would have friends, you'd best be friendly. But, you say, "I'm shy, retiring; I don't meet people easily. It's just not possible for me to be a friend. I was born an introvert and am most likely to stay that way."

I'm not suggesting you attempt to alter your personality or to pretend to be what you are not. One solution might be to start by being a friend to other introverts. Even better, I'd be willing to bet you have within you an untapped source of "friend-making ability" that if nurtured and encouraged could literally change your life. It all starts by recognizing the principle that it really does take time to understand one another.

The powerful, provocative thinker and writer, Elie Wiesel, in *Souls on Fire,* makes a powerful statement that may be just the tonic for you. He reflects that when we die and go to meet our Maker, we're not going to be asked why we didn't become a messiah or find a cure for cancer. Instead we will be asked, Why didn't you become you? What a great question. "Becoming you" includes both the joy and the privilege of learning to recognize the marvelous differences that exist in those around you.

Will it take time? Yes, it will. Will it require work? Absolutely. Who is responsible if it doesn't happen? Jack Parr once said something that answers that. He quipped, "My life seems like one long obstacle course, with me as the chief obstacle." Isn't that generally true of us all? Could it be you are standing in the way of your own good progress when it comes to taking the time to work at understanding the people who surround you? If that is true, wouldn't this be a good time to do something about it, and reach out to someone as a friend?

No Pain, No Gain

I'm convinced one of the major obstacles to accepting the differences in our friends and acquaintances is that we're afraid to make even the tiniest mistake in interpersonal relationships. No one wants to make a fool out of himself or herself; that goes without saying. Somehow we often feel our humanity will be all too glaring if we make the slightest *faux pax,* as if people didn't already know we were human.

It's no disgrace to make a mistake. The real tragedy comes in working so hard at being perfect that you never let the world around you know who you really are. If you never let people get to know you—and if you never take the time to truly get to know them—you'll never understand those whom you want as friends. It will take time to develop mutual trust and understanding. Anything worth attaining, especially friendships, will always take time. But nothing significant is likely to happen until you take that first tentative step. You'll be surprised how the other steps fall right in line. The best news of all is that most of this can take place *in your own* back yard.

Some stories have such a ring of truth and say it so beautifully and so well that they live forever in our memories. One such story is called "Acres of Diamonds." No one knows exactly where the story was first told or who told it. It may not even be true, but its actual history is incidental to the truth of the tale.

We do know, however, who made the story famous. Dr.

Russell Herman Conwell (1843–1925) covered the length and breadth of the United States, telling and retelling this amazing story. It's been said he told it more than six thousand times and attracted the attention of literally millions of people. The money he raised from his lectures—totaling some $6 million—was used to found Temple University in Philadelphia, thus bringing to reality his dream of building a first-class university for poor but deserving young people who would otherwise be unable to attend college.

The story is about a farmer in Africa during the years when the first diamonds were being discovered there. The promise of great wealth intrigued the farmer, and one day he could no longer restrain his insatiable desire for wealth. He sold his farm and set off in search of the diamonds that would make him a wealthy, happy man.

His search was long and painful. He wandered throughout the African continent but all to no avail. He found no diamonds. Finally, penniless, unwell, and utterly discouraged, he took his life by throwing himself into a raging river.

Some time before this, however, the man who bought the farmer's land found a large, strange-looking stone in the small creek that ran across his farm. He placed it on his mantel as a curio.

Later, a visitor came to the farmer's home. Seeing the unusual stone over the fireplace, he turned to the new owner of the farm and informed him that he had found one of the largest diamonds ever known to man. Further investigation revealed the entire farm was literally covered with similar magnificent stones. In fact, this farm sold by the first farmer so that he could travel the continent in search of great wealth turned out to be one of the richest, most productive diamond mines in the world.

After telling this story, Dr. Conwell would then make the point that had already become obvious. The first farmer owned literally millions of diamonds, and they were in his own back yard. He simply had not taken the time to investigate what he had.

I believe it's often the same way with friendships. First, it's going to take time to discover where the diamonds of friendship really are. Initially, they may not look like diamonds at all. In fact, they may appear to be anything but diamonds. (Remember my negative attitude toward my friend Don Odle mentioned in chapter 1.) But stay with them. Nurture them. Give of yourself to them.

Second, it will take time to develop those relationships into friendships that have the stuff to last a lifetime. It will not happen overnight. It's much like a long-term investment. You don't get ten years of interest for one month's deposit. It's not that way in business or friendship.

What about the diamonds of friendship scattered about in your back yard? Are you walking over untold riches every day because you haven't made the effort to see what is really there? If that is true, slow down, take a good look, invest the time necessary to get to know those you say you care about.

Where do you start? A good place is right in your own home, at the office, in your church. Scores of people all around you are crying out for someone to be their friend. Visit an elderly shut-in down the block, spend some time with a prisoner, or talk an hour or two with a youngster who's struggling with the loneliness and sadness of parents who have divorced. In the process, you won't so much *find* happiness; on the contrary, you will discover that *happiness has found you*!

The writer Catherine Marshall tells of a husband and

wife who moved to a new area where they knew no one. They had no friends, no relatives. As a result, they became increasingly irritable and unhappy with each other. Nothing seemed to be going right.

Then one day the couple befriended a waitress who apologized to them for slow service. She too was new in town and very unhappy. They invited her to their home after work. Before long, other people were asked to join in the visits, which grew into a project called "Adventures in Caring." As Catherine Marshall notes, "This couple soon became so concerned with the needs of others that their life was enriched beyond anything I can describe. Happiness found them."[3]

Has happiness found you yet? Have you begun to double your possibilities for joy by extending your hand, your heart of friendship? You can, and you can start right now. Don't be discouraged when it takes your energies, patience, and time. Friendships to last a lifetime will require long hours, days, and months of kindness, nurturing, listening, and compassion. The payoff is tremendous, and part of that great joy of a long-term friendship is the constant discovery of the many mysteries that reside in the heart of your friend.

Isn't there someone close by who needs your friendship? Are you willing to make the effort and take the time to make it happen? I hope so. It's an absolutely vital principle to remember and put into practice when it comes to being a friend.

Listen to me for a day—an hour!—a moment.
Lest I expire in my terrible wilderness, my
lonely silence! O God, is there no one to listen?
—Seneca (4 B.C.)

LEARN TO LISTEN!

In chapter three, we talked about the importance of taking the time to develop relationships—the ones that have the potential to become truly great friendships. Without that time, effort, sweat, and tears, we could well miss out on life's greatest blessings. I know, because it almost happened to me right in my own living room.

It was a cold, rainy night. My son Gordon, now thirty-eight years old but then twenty-one, finally came home around 1:00 A.M. after a long night of smoking marijuana with his friends. I was livid, embarrassed, distraught, and afraid. How could this young man whom we loved so much do this to his mother and me? It wasn't fair; it wasn't right. It was happening to other parents, but who would have ever thought it would have reared its ugly head in the Engstrom family?

We couldn't understand why. But this particular evening I held my peace, even though I had a mind to give Gordon a tongue lashing he would never forget. I listened to him as he shouted that most Christians were phonies, the church was filled with hypocrites, and there were at least a hundred ways to God. On and on he went.

The more I listened, the more something began to happen inside me. After a while, I no longer saw a son whose head was clouded from the effects of pot. Instead, I began to hear him. Even though I didn't—and don't—approve of anyone's ingesting drugs for recreational purposes, I knew that much of what Gordon had to say was true. There is a tremendous absence of love for each other within the body of Christ. Too often our lifestyles do bear little resemblance to that of the Man from Galilee. And yes, Christians are not perfect, and no, they don't all know how to be friends.

I can remember a hot tear falling on my cheek, then another and another as Gordon spoke. I knew in my heart of hearts he was also talking about me. I only tell you this story to say this. Although that winter evening in January 1968 was difficult, humiliating, and upsetting, I think it may have been the first night I really listened to Gordon. In a fresh, new way, I was establishing a real relationship with my son. It was something that changed my life—our lives. It was the beginning of what has now become a beautiful friendship.

Is There No One Who Will Listen?

It's been called a fine art, an uncommon personal skill that must be practiced, developed, and nurtured. It's also been referred to as the most difficult thing for most people to do. Yet, for meaningful, effective living—and to ensure lifelong friendships—it is something we neglect at our own peril.

I'm talking about the ability to listen. The French writer, Pascal, said, "We only consult the ear because the heart is waiting." Shakespeare wrote, "Give every man thine ear, but few thy voice." A modern sales representative reminds his sales staff: "When you're telling, you're not selling." Listening! How important! How very difficult! John Drakeford gives us these thoughts on listening.

- Poor listening is responsible for a tremendous waste in education, industry, and many other areas of life.
- Any capable democratic leader can immeasurably improve his effectiveness by cultivating a listening ear.
- Time spent in listening plays a vital part in building good relationships with people.
- Marriages that are sick can often be strengthened when husbands and wives will learn to listen to each other.
- As we listen to people we help them break out of their skin-enclosed isolation and enter into the community of experience and discover their potential.
- All forms of psychotherapy emphasize that listening is probably the most simple and effective single technique for helping troubled people.[1]

All of these statements should tell us everyone is looking for a friendly ear. Therefore, the next principle can be stated:

---

4. Commit yourself to learning how to listen.

It may be a furrowed brow, a grimace that speaks volumes, a hard swallow, or a sigh that simply says "I hear you, I understand, and I think I know what you're going through"—all are part of what it means to listen. It's absolutely amazing what we can do without saying a word. Conversely, it can be devastating to everyone concerned when we hear only what we want to hear. A personal example will illustrate this fact.

A man well known in Christian circles was being accused of homosexuality. The rumors were flying of his sexual exploits both at home and abroad. No one had yet proved anything, but it seemed as if the allegations had every reason to be true. I believed them, and when I finally brought the man into my office, I unloaded both barrels. I judged him, I spoke harshly, I was so relentless in my attack that he quickly found himself painted into a corner from which there was no possible escape.

I was so certain I was right that I didn't bother to listen to him. I knew I was right, and I knew he had done wrong. That is, until the truth emerged some weeks later that every rumor had been untrue. He was not, nor had he ever been, a homosexual.

Those are the painful lessons that come with not listening. But there is a better way, and one of the great masters of the theater is our example.

Perhaps you've had the privilege of seeing him perform. He is the amazing, renowned French mime, Marcel Marceau. He speaks four languages and could easily hold his own on just about any subject imaginable, but every year he chooses to perform before hundreds of thousands of awestruck fans in absolute silence.

Marceau's facial expression of anguish is more graphic than if he had taken ten minutes to tell you in words the pain he feels. When in his performance he accepts a loving gift from a friend, his whole body says thank you. Marceau can make you laugh, cry, feel anger, pity, or remorse by the skillful display of simple, subtle facial and body movements.

He has often explained his phenomenal success by saying that people simply want to be communicated with, and his pantomimes never fail to break through barriers of culture, language, and what would otherwise be human misunderstanding.

When Marceau first came to the United States from France, would-be promoters who saw his act said, "No sex, no scenery and he doesn't say a word? It will never be commercial."[2] That just goes to show how wrong agents can be! For someone with the time-proven performing skills of a Marcel Marceau, the absence of sex and scenery and the presence of silence have hardly been detrimental to his career.

As I found myself reading story after story of this amazing showman (and I encourage you to see him perform whenever you have the opportunity), I couldn't help thinking about the untapped power of silence that could do so much good in our lives, if we would only let it. It's common knowledge that virtually every high school and college in the land has a course in public speaking, but we would be hard pressed to find in the curriculum many classes on how to listen or how to express our deepest feelings without saying a word. Yet, these are precisely the skills each of us must develop if we are to learn how to become a friend.

Marcel Marceau has nonverbal skills few of us will ever match. In fact, many of us speak more loudly with our bodies than with words. In his book, *More Communication Keys to Your Marriage,* H. Norman Wright, nationally known and respected lecturer, marriage counselor, and author, asks us to give two or three responses to a list of "non-verbal/non-voice behaviors." I found this exercise fascinating and helpful.

Take a few minutes and see what responses you come up with. Read each item on the following list and try to give two or three "meanings" to each behavior. "Listen" to what you see here:

a. A child nods his head up and down.
b. A person turns her head rapidly in a certain direction.
c. A person smiles slightly.
d. A person's lower lip quivers slightly.
e. A person speaks in a loud, harsh voice.
f. A person speaks in a low, monotonous voice.
g. A person suddenly opens his eyes wide.
h. A person keeps her eyes lowered as she speaks to you.
i. A person speaks in a very halting or hesitant voice.
j. A person yawns during a conversation.
k. A person shrugs his shoulders.[3]

After you've done this exercise, give it to your spouse, your children, or a friend or colleague. See how your individual responses differ. I think you'll discover a whole new communication awareness. At the same time you'll unearth another powerful way to respond to the needs of your friend as you develop your skills of observing and listening without ears.

How to Ruin a Friendship in One Easy Lesson

It was a Friday. The time was 2:30 A.M. Two of our close friends I will call Pete and Joan Johnson were sleeping soundly when Joan heard a noise outside their window. She rose to check on the strange sounds only to discover the neighbor's cat sharpening her claws on their shake roof. Joan started to return to bed when she felt faint. Before she knew it, she had fallen to the floor, limp and immobilized. Somehow she was able to call to her husband, "Help me, help me." Pete woke up to find his wife lying shivering in the darkness, unable to move.

Pete took Joan in his arms and placed her on the bed. He turned on the light to discover his wife's body had by now gone completely limp and her eyes had rolled back up into her head. In panic, Pete rushed to the medicine cabinet and returned with a ten-year-old bottle of smelling salts he hoped still had some potency. They did. He slapped at Joan's face and gave her nostrils a hefty dose of pungent salts. Startled, she opened her eyes. After a few minutes it was apparent she would be all right. But for those few brief moments, Pete thought he had lost his dear wife.

Pete and Joan had been invited to dinner the next evening with very good friends, but they both felt it would be better if they stayed home. The trauma of the early morning was still too much to deal with. They knew that rest and relaxation were more appropriate than having to talk loudly for three hours in a noisy restaurant. Besides, they wanted to be sure Joan was all right.

Joan called and spoke to the woman who had invited them. Joan said she had fainted that morning and Pete was afraid she had died. They felt it would be best to take a rain check on the evening.

Without missing a beat, Joan's friend quipped, "Oh, that's nothing. I've fainted lots of times. Now, when can we get together? I mean I was really counting on you two coming. The Michaels will be there, and so will the Wilsons."

Joan then said quietly, "But Pete was really afraid that I was gone." To which her friend said, "Oh, well, I've never had quite that experience. But I've fainted lots of times. Now let's get our datebooks out and set a new time for dinner."

To hear Joan tell it, it was one of the most devastating conversations she ever had with her friend. There were no listening, no compassion, no concerned silence—none of the responses you would expect from a true friend. At that moment a blow was struck at the friendship. Perhaps it will not be a fatal blow, at least I hope not. But it hurt. It cut deeply.

For whatever reason, Joan's friend forgot one of the most vital ingredients in a friendship is being there to listen at any time of the day or night. It's good for us to listen to stories such as these, because if we observe ourselves in our busy, day-to-day activities we may discover we are often overly preoccupied with our own concerns to hear the needs of a friend. I have one friend in particular who is never too busy to talk to me. And he is one of the busiest men in America.

During one of the more difficult early years of my association with World Vision, I made more than one attempt to extricate myself from the virtually unmanageable fiscal problems and personality conflicts that were daily dogging my steps. In short, I wanted to resign. I was determined to get out. I felt I could no longer cope with the problems.

I went to my friend Dick Halverson, chairman of the World Vision board—and now chaplain of the United States Senate—and I was as direct as I've ever been in my entire life. I said I was through—finished. He looked me straight in the eye and said, "Oh, no, you're not. You've just begun. Besides, if you leave, it will be the death of World Vision."

I doubt the truth of that last statement, but one thing was

certain. Dick did not approve of my decision. I listened, he listened, we cried, we prayed, and I stayed.

On yet another occasion Dorothy and I made plans for a long weekend with our dear friends Bette and Ned Vessey. I needed to get away just to think and pray—again about my future relationship with World Vision. I'm not normally one to walk away from a challenge, but the pressures, the uncertainties, the personality conflicts were becoming too much to bear.

I told Ned I wanted out, that I simply could not manage the affairs of World Vision any longer. Ned listened. He would nod his head, purse his lips, perhaps shift his feet a bit as he sat there. But he said nothing, not a single word. I just talked and talked. Ned listened and listened.

Hours later when I was all through talking, and when I figured Ned was probably through listening, an uncommon wave of peace came over my heart. I found myself not wanting to leave World Vision at all. If anything, my spirit was renewed, my faith rekindled, hope was restored, and I was a new man. I resolved not to resign, and I was prepared to pour my very best into my work. All Ned had done was listen.

I'm not suggesting every outcome will be the same for you as it was for me during those critical hours. I do know the staying power of a friend's listening ear can help restore perspective to what may be little more than mass confusion.

"Smile and Let the Talk Wash Over"

As I started to write this chapter I noticed a copy of *Sports Illustrated* on my desk. I take a degree of pride in staying up-to-date with current theological books, missions articles, and a variety of magazines that help me to keep abreast of world events. I must confess, when *Sports Illustrated* arrives, I put many of those other journals aside to bury myself in that week's exploits of our nation's greatest athletes. Today was no different.

The headline on the cover read: "Sportswoman of the Year." One of the pictures below showed Mary Decker pressing the tape as she defeated—by inches—the Soviet champion, Zamira Zaitseva, in a 1500 meters world championship race. The article went on to describe her phenomenal performances in San Diego, Los Angeles, Gateshead (England), Stockholm, Paris, and Oslo.

I was particularly struck by one comment made about Mary by the writer of the article. He wrote, "She can be demanding. She can be shyly coy. She can show an explosive temper. *She can sit all evening at the feet of a friend and not say anything, just smile and let the talk wash over her*" (italics mine).[4]

Those last words hit me between the eyes. What a wonderful way to put it. Have you ever done that—just let the "talk wash over"? If you have, you know the joy that comes from this kind of maximum friendship. After all, when you are with your best friend there is little need to rely on nonstop conversation. Often it will be enough to smile, listen, and let the talk wash over you. Ultimately, this quiet, intentional listening may even turn an adversary into a friend. It happened to me.

It's been said that experience is what you get when you were expecting something else. When we translate that into relationships, it reads something like: I thought we would always be friends. Never in my wildest dreams did I ever think this friendship would end. Yet the years prove to all of us that friends do come and go. People we worked with, played with, and even prayed with at some point are no longer close to us. Some even become adversaries. There is a way to deal with this most difficult situation. I experienced this in my up and down relationship with the founder of World Vision, Bob Pierce.

I first met Bob at a Youth for Christ Conference in Medicine Lake, Minnesota, at the second annual conference of YFC. I was taken to him immediately, and we began what would become a long friendship. I was next with him at the great World Congress on Evangelism in Beatenberg, Switzerland, in 1948. During that time he was carrying on his missionary activities and evangelism in China. It was also the time when he wrote in his Bible, "Let my heart be broken with the things that break the heart of God," which became his life's slogan.

Bob and Dr. Frank C. Phillips then organized World Vision officially as an incorporated body in 1950. During those early years I was very close to Bob Pierce. I was a frequent guest in his home, and I often spoke on his Mutual Network radio broadcast in California. Bob also came to our home in Wheaton, Illinois, on numerous occasions. We would talk, pray, laugh, and enjoy each other to the point where our friendship fast became one of supreme importance to both of us.

In 1963 when I resigned as president of Youth for Christ International, Bob invited me to meet with the World Vision Board of Directors. I was invited to become vice-president of World Vision. Bob said the Lord had laid my name on his heart, and he asked me if I would be willing to consider coming with him in this new role. I told him I wasn't sure, but I would certainly pray about it. After meeting twice with the World Vision board, I accepted their invitation to become executive vice-president of the organization. It was September 1963. When I came with World Vision, I knew there were obstacles and challenges to Bob Pierce's vision, but I was unaware just how great some of those obstacles were. I soon learned World Vision was in deep financial trouble. We had over $440,000 in debts hanging over our heads from the great Tokyo Crusade Bob had directed. We were also falling behind about $30,000 each month with Bob's radio broadcasts (which was a lot of money in those days—and still is!).

I revealed these realities to the board at a special meeting in Laguna Beach, California, in the fall of 1963. Bob was smitten, literally upended at my report. He asked for a leave of absence, which was granted by the board. For the next year, I was instructed to do all I could to bring some order out of what I sensed was absolute chaos.

"A Root of Bitterness"

Bob never forgave me for what he said was my "stealing" of his organization and for "taking him off the air." There were tremendous tensions, angry words, and unpleasant encounters for that entire one year—tensions that continued when Bob returned for his final two years as president of World Vision.

Later, Bob Pierce resigned, but he did so with what he said was "bitterness in his heart." He continued to hold me responsible for his leaving. Our friendship seemed to be on its last legs. That was in 1968.

In 1973, I was in Africa conducting World Vision business when I received a cable from Bob. He referred to his "root of bitterness" in the cable. He asked if we could meet together upon my return home. I cabled him immediately and said I would call him the hour I returned to Los Angeles, which I did.

The next day, Bob and I met at noon at the Derby Restaurant near the World Vision offices. We parted at five o'clock. We looked each other over in the eye as we shared our hurts and fears, wept, and listened to each other as we had never listened before. We prayed until we could pray no more, listened until we could listen no more, with the one theme of our prayer being that our hearts would be reunited. It was the most exhausting personal encounter I've ever known, but during those five hours Bob and I began to understand many of the problems basic to our separation.

I had thought, when I came to California, that I was coming as Bob Pierce's friend. He saw me coming as his employee and the person to assist him in running the organization. When we really started listening to each other, we discovered each of us had an entirely different concept of what my role was to be.

As we sat across from each other for those five hours in that restaurant, we finally cleared the air that paved the way for reconciliation. Although our friendship was never again blessed with the openness and beauty of those earlier years, we had done what was necessary to restore the relationship. From that day forward Bob and I were able to be comfortable with each other right up to the day he went to be with the Lord.

I deeply loved Bob Pierce, and even though the hurts were on both sides of the friendship, I know in the end there was an equal amount of mutual affection. There is no question that Bob was the most complex person I've ever known. But World Vision could never have become what it has become over the years without the drive, dream, and energy that Bob brought to everything he did.

For both Bob and me, turning an adversary into a friend took hours of praying and weeping. It took a mutual choosing to listen, to love, and to trust one another once again, but it was worth every single struggling minute of it.

The key word here is *choose*. The restoration of a friendship *never* comes about automatically, nor can it ever be unilateral. It takes the willingness to be uncompromisingly open. It requires total commitment on both sides that says, "We want our friendship to be all it can be." Above all it demands the courtesy of listening.

Originality is simply a pair of fresh eyes.
—*T. H. Higginson*

5

"BEING THERE"

In the preceding chapter we saw that taking the time to listen at great lengths is quite possibly one of the most powerful of all principles when it comes to being a friend. Some of that listening is active; much of it is listening without saying a word. But there's still another dimension to friendship that can be every bit as powerful. You've been there, and so have I.

In 1968 I had to enter a Boston hospital for a hip rehabilitation operation. My wife, Dorothy, my friends, and all my associates were in California. That was not a very comforting thought for me as I was preparing to enter surgery so many miles away from home.

Then the most amazing thing happened. Within twelve hours, not only was Dorothy at my side but so were two of our closest friends from home, Ned and Bette Vessey. This couple had taken time from their busy work schedule and other pressing obligations to be at my side during what was to be a serious operation.

I can still remember my feelings, and I can still feel those tears that streamed down my cheeks as I lay in my hospital bed looking into the faces of these precious people who loved me enough to travel the breadth of the nation to be at my side. But Ned and Bette did not care only about me! They checked into Boston's Parker House Hotel so they could be in close contact with Dorothy who had a room in that hotel. They took her to breakfast, lunch, and dinner. They sat with her for long hours in the hospital waiting room. They talked with her, prayed with her, and I wouldn't be surprised if Bette didn't do some occasional shopping with Dorothy.

I don't think I've had an experience before or since that has been a more precise definition of what it means to be there. You see, it wasn't what my friends said, the flowers they sent, or the messages of comfort they wrote. It was their physical presence. They cared enough to send their very best—themselves—to my side. My friendship with them was already deep. After that Boston experience, it became profound.

Being There When It Counts

Not long ago a prominent Christian leader and long-time friend called and said he needed to spend some time with me immediately. When would I be in Chicago? I told him I was planning to be there the day after next, and I agreed to meet him. My friend flew eight hundred miles for that meeting, and for three hours we talked and intimately shared in a secluded corner of the American Airlines Admiral Lounge at O'Hare Airport.

This man is much more well known than I, but for the purposes of our meeting that didn't matter. It was enough that we were friends. We had already been through many "acid tests" of our friendship in the past where we both took the kinds of risks that could have sent our relationship in any number of directions. Now, we were comfortable just being there and being friends.

As we talked, we commented on a television commercial for the phone company we had seen over and over. Each of us identified with it so closely that it became a long subject of conversation. It was about two men who in spite of the passage of many years were "still there" for each other.

Perhaps you've seen the spot. A portly monsignor is walking reverently through the solitude of his monastery, when a young priest rushes up and whispers to him that he has a phone call in his office. The caller's name is Will, he says, apparently "an old football buddy."

The senior priest does his best to maintain a dignified posture but obviously can hardly contain his delight as he hurries back to his office. The conversation between the two old friends is brief, but it's enough. After so many years, the two men are reliving the experiences of their youth. Will asks the monsignor if he thinks he can still catch a pass. The monsignor says, "Yes, Will, if you can still throw one." The two aging football players didn't need many more words than that. Those kinds of friendships seldom need words. All that mattered was that each was simply there for the other.

Then, as they finish their conversation appropriate music accompanies the moves of the camera as it pans old, faded football pictures on the monsignor's desk. The wry smile and hint of a tear on the monsignor's face say it all. The tag line is a reminder to the viewer to stay in touch with old friends. It was a beautiful moment, and a commercial I'm glad the phone company produced.

Effective Rx for Friendship

Author, editor, and critic, Norman Cousins, now professor of medical humanities at the School of Medicine, the University of California at Los Angeles, tells his own story of being there that bears repeating here. It's about a group of men and women at a California VA hospital, all of whom were dying of cancer. Cousins had been invited by the doctors to speak to these patients in hopes of brightening their spirits. It's best to let Norman Cousins himself tell the story.

> The patients sat in front of me in about seven rows. There were about 60 or 70 of them. I suggested...what was known about the human brain and spoke about laughter, because some medical researchers believe that laughter helps to stimulate the endorphins and helps the brain to write its prescriptions.

Cousins went on to tell stories and jokes, and even had a laughter sound track to create an atmosphere of hilarity. "After about five or six minutes, it was difficult for the people to stay in their seats, and out of mercy I had to stop. Then I asked them how they felt. The interesting thing that happened was that while they were laughing, their pain had disappeared."

Cousins then suggested they accept the responsibility for creating their own programs by putting on one-act plays and other productions. He also said they might want to buy video- and audiocassettes of stand-up comics and other forms of uplifting entertainment. He then said his good-byes and left. But Cousins later returned to this hospital where he found a different atmosphere from that of his first visit.

When I came back seven weeks later, the doctors told me that they had noticed they were getting much better results. The atmosphere had changed. The people were hopeful, and they became partners in the enterprise. But equally important to me was the fact that the morale of the doctors had been boosted too.

When I came back the second time, the patients were no longer sitting in rows, as they were the first time. They had devised a different format for their meetings. Now they sat in one large circle, so everyone could see everyone else. Also, sitting in a circle enabled them to be joined to one another. And the doctors were not sitting up here, the way they did before, on the platform, with the patients sitting out there. Now the doctors were interspersed in the group.

No longer were these people seeing themselves as victims of a dreaded disease. Instead, they had energized and revitalized themselves to such a degree that virtually every day was nothing short of a celebration. Cousins continued, "When they began each meeting, each person had to say what it was that was good that had happened to him or her since the last meeting. And the dependence of the group on having something good happen to each of its members was so strong, no one wanted to turn up empty-handed."

One woman told her fellow patients her nephew had just been admitted to medical school. He had written a letter to her, saying, "Just hang in there, Auntie, and tell your friends to do the same. I'm going to come up with the answer."

A Korean War veteran reported he had received a telephone call from a buddy he hadn't seen since the end of the Korean War. The stories of "what was good" abounded as each patient told his or her story. Why? Because one day one man—Norman Cousins—had taken the time to spend a few hours in being a friend to people who had lost all hope. He had chosen simply to be there, and being there had made all the difference.[1]

Cousins reminded us the most profound things are profoundly simple. That's why this next principle of friendship is vital.

---

5. Simply be there to care, whether you know exactly what to do or not.

Apostle to the Unwanted

Mother Teresa, that remarkable, tireless woman in Calcutta whose life and work reflect the epitome of caring for the destitute and the dying, is surely our greatest contemporary example of what it means to do something "beautiful for God." I am moved again and again when I read of what she does to touch people in need. Malcom Muggeridge wrote reflectively about the Calcutta he saw in the company of Mother Teresa.

> The biggest disease today is not leprosy or tuberculosis, but rather the feeling of being unwanted, uncared for and deserted by everybody. The greatest evil is the lack of love and charity, the terrible indifference towards one's neighbor who lives at the roadside assaulted by exploitation, corruption, poverty and disease.[2]

Among the most profound human words ever spoken of what it means to be a friend are these from the lips of Mother Teresa herself—Calcutta's "Angel of Mercy":

When I was homeless, you opened your doors,
When I was naked, you gave me your coat,

When I was weary, you helped me find rest,
When I was anxious, you calmed all my fears,

When I was little, you taught me to read,
When I was lonely, you gave me your love,

When in a prison, you came to my cell,
When on sick bed, you cared for my needs,

In a strange country, you made me at home,
Seeking employment, you found me a job,

Hurt in a battle, you bound up my wounds,
Searching for kindness, you held out your hand,

When I was Negro, or Chinese, or White,
Mocked and insulted you carried my cross,

When I was aged, you bothered to smile,
When I was restless, you listened and cared,

You saw me covered with spittle and blood,
You knew my features, though grimy with sweat,

When I was laughed at, you stood by my side,
When I was happy, you shared in my joy.[3]

Is there someone you can think of at this very moment
who needs to know that you are willing to be there to care?
Perhaps it's even as close to home as a spouse, a child, a parent; it could be an old classmate, your pastor, a colleague in
the office. It doesn't need to be a person suffering on the
streets of Calcutta. What is required of us is to put down
our roots, grow, and blossom where we are planted. Pray for
the spirit of friendship to take root and grow in your heart,
right where you are.

One day the newspaper reporter took out his pad and pencil, looked the fabulously wealthy J. Paul Getty in the eye, and asked, "Mr. Getty, what is it that money cannot buy?" Getty replied, "I don't think it can buy health, and I don't think it can buy a good time. Some of the best times I have ever had didn't cost any money."

Wouldn't you agree that some of the most effective and meaningful manifestations of friendship cost us little or nothing in money? There are hundreds, probably thousands of situations where our money is no good. And if money could buy them or fix them, we would be hard pressed to attach an appropriate price tag.

After twenty-five years of marriage a wife falls victim to a spreading, debilitating cancer. How much is a letter from a friend that's filled with sorrow and prayers worth to the grieving husband? $100? $5000? $100,000? None of the above. "Being there" was all that mattered.

An elderly friend who lives alone loses her job, and for the first time in her life she is panic-stricken at the gut-wrenching awareness that she no longer has any means of support. What is it worth to her to know that you will remain her friend, standing by, helping, doing what you can for her as long as it's necessary? It probably means just about everything.

A young couple is filled with the pride and joy that come with the arrival of a first child. They have spared no expense for cuddly teddy bears, special clothes, ribbons, and bows. A rocking chair for the new mother is lovingly placed near the window. The parents' love for their precious baby is all-consuming. Then one night all is too silent in the crib. The child doesn't wake for her bottle. The worst has happened. Crib death has snatched their tiny treasure. At this terrible time in their lives, what value can be placed on a friend who comes to weep with them and remains available day or night? A friend who will simply be there? Obviously, the money in the banks of all the oil sheiks combined would not be enough. There are some things you and I cannot buy, because some things—and usually the best things—are not for sale. Friendship is one of those things. But some people won't risk friendship.

Often I ask people who admit they are lonely and void of companionship why they feel they have no friends. The usual answer is, "I just don't feel I could measure up to what someone else might expect of me. I have too many limitations."

On a recent cross-country flight Harold Wilke of White Plains, New York, noticed the hostess giving him strange glances every time she walked by him. Finally, the young lady spoke up, "Sir, you're wearing your watch on your ankle!"

"It's the latest style," said Harold, smiling. She nodded and went on with her work only to return a few minutes later to say, "I'm sorry. I didn't notice you were handicapped. I hope I didn't offend you." Harold assured her she had not. Instead Harold said, "In fact, I like to have my imagination noticed."

Harold was born with no arms, but his parents always taught him to make the best of what was available. Harold has his feet, so that is what he uses. He types with his feet, writes with his feet, drives with his feet, and—to the hostess's surprise—wears his watch on his ankle.

Harold Wilke has refused to be curtailed by his limitations. Here's what Harold has to tell us:

1. *Find underdeveloped resources.* He reminds us that our minds, like our bodies, often produce only a trickle of their potential because we don't exercise them. (Harold can swim with the best of them.)

2. *Focus on the solution, not the problem.* He asks us to be-

lieve that a limitation or disability is not as important as what we do about it. Harold says, "God sees you and me, even with our limitations, as whole persons; we've been given power to overcome our predicaments. We have limitless resources to find *different* answers."

3. *Wake up your "third eye."* To Harold this means to use your imagination. In other words, if you don't have a wrist, wear your watch on your ankle. Harold has a word for us all: "Stuck with a limitation? Is something holding you back? Know what I've discovered? You can always find another way."[4]

When I read that story, I photocopied it and sent it with a short note to several of those people who had told me, "I'm afraid to make friends because of my limitations." Do you know what? It helped them.

One of those friendless people sent me a fast reply that read:

Dear Ted,
Those two pages written by Harold Wilke made me ashamed of the attitude I've been carrying all these years. I've really missed out on the goldmine of friendship because I thought I'd have to be the "perfect" friend. Well I guess I don't want to believe that anymore, and as a result, my life's taken on a whole new excitement. I'm realizing for the first time that I don't have to *do* anything special to be a friend. The most important thing is just "to be there"—just being available and accessible. Limitations? What limitations? Thanks for helping me get off dead center.
—ML

Are you paying too much heed to your limitations? If you are, take Harold Wilke's advice to heart. Focus on the solution, not the problem. You'll be pleasantly surprised to discover you have all you need inside yourself right now to develop the fine art of friendship. Don't worry about what you have to *do*. Instead, concentrate on *being there*. It will change your life.

A Permanent Friend in an Unstable World

For more than thirty-five years I've kept one special little poem in a file in my desk. It is my personal reminder of how easy it is to get sucked up in the speed, technology, and craziness of the age—all at the expense of relationships.

> This is the age
> Of the half-read page.
> And the quick hash
> And the mad dash.
> The bright night
> With the nerves tight.
> The plane hop
> With the brief stop.
> The lamp tan
> In a short span.
> The Big Shot
> In a good spot.
> And the brain strain
> And the heart pain.
> And the cat naps
> Till the spring snaps—
> And the fun's done!
> —Virginia Brasier[5]

Now, a third of a century after that poem was written, we live in a time when men and women know more about computers than they do about caring. It's an age when we are still more familiar with keeping up with the Joneses than we are with keeping up with Jesus. We seem to be more concerned about Big Brother than we are about the righteousness of God the Father.

For many of us the brain strain and the heart pain will finally force that spring to snap after which we'll be compelled to admit the fun's truly done. By then it will be too late, and we'll have to say in our heart of hearts that it really wasn't any fun after all. Where do we turn to get all this back in perspective?

Never has there been a greater model for friendship than Jesus Christ. Jesus was always there when He was needed. Strong, stable, caring, He touched everyone He met at his or her own private level of need—the woman at the well, Nicodemus, Zaccheus, the woman taken in adultery, the disciples with all their confused, misguided thinking. There was even a special word to the rich young ruler. To those who suffered physical affliction Jesus not only spoke but also healed. Jesus was a friend to all while He physically walked our earth. The miracle of all miracles is that the Incarnation continues in the lives of His people today. He is still that friend who sticks closer than a brother.

He is a permanent, unchanging friend in a world that steers itself on a wildly swerving collision course with the future. As we immerse ourselves in His boundless love, He gives us the thrill of being surprised by an unspeakable joy. He gives us the courage to re-examine our views. He somehow makes it easy for us to admit that we don't yet understand a thing. He upsets our tidy, carefully designed prisons and sets before us mansions of grace and beauty.

All the time He is saying, "I will never leave you or forsake you." Right now He wants to help you and me turn our troubles into triumphs, our failures into faith, and our mental and spiritual paralysis into limitless possibilities for good. He also wants us to be His hands, His feet, His heart to men and women, boys and girls who don't have a friend...to be there to care when we're needed most. It's one of the most simple, yet most profound, principles of all when it comes to learning the fine art of friendship.

6

*A great many people think they are
thinking when they are really rearranging
their prejudices and superstitions.*
—*Edward R. Murrow*

LOOK FOR THE UNLIKELY

It was 7:00 A.M., May 1979. Pat Moore, who looked like she must be eighty-five years old, opened the door of her New York apartment and stepped nervously into the hall. Ready to embark on one of the strangest trips of her life, she put her cane out in front of her and hesitantly felt for the first step on the stairs. The only thoughts in her mind were, *Can I do it? Can I make this work?*

Her legs moved gingerly, awkwardly. One step...two, three...all the way to the twelfth step. So far so good. When she arrived at the bottom of the stairs, she saw her landlady who exclaimed, "Oh, I'm sorry, I was expecting somebody else."

"Don't you recognize me?" said Pat, her voice strained and cracked.

"No, ma'am, I don't," said the landlady, staring at the frail woman.

"I'm Pat Moore," she said, laughing. As she saw her landlady's mouth widen in disbelief, Pat knew in that flash of a moment she passed the test.

You see, Pat Moore was not eighty-five years old at all. Not even close. She was an attractive twenty-six-year-old specialist in industrial design, with a deep concern for how we are responding to the practical needs of the aged in our society.

For at least once each week for the next three years, "eighty-five-year-old" Pat put on her masquerade of facial latex foam, a heavy fabric that bound her body, and a convincing gray wig. She visited fourteen states as an old woman. She met hundreds of people who never once discovered her true identity.

One of the first suspicions she settled was her initial feeling that older people are ignored simply because they are old. Pat Moore's story of being old is absolutely one of the most fascinating accounts of personal identity I've ever read.[1]

Remember the old saying that we never really know the needs of another until we've walked a mile in his or her moccasins? That is precisely what Pat Moore did for thirty-six months. She developed such a sensitivity for the aged in our midst that she actually started to "feel" old. Her experiment was the consummate definition of complete identification with others.

Pat's successful attempt to get in touch with the needs of the aged is a living example of the sixth vital principle in learning and living the fine art of friendship.

---

6. Always treat others as equals.

This principle obviously does not apply only to the aged. There also needs to be a greater sense of mutual respect among the races, the sexes, our competitors, and our bosses or employees. To neglect this principle is to be ignorant of what others have to offer our own tired spirits. In discussing equality, I'm not saying all people will have the same gifts, abilities, I.Q.'s, talents, or views of life. They won't, and that is what makes friendship so exciting. But would we not live wiser, happier, and more fulfilled lives if we enjoyed each other for what the other person is? Young or old, black or white, rich or poor, adult or child? Treating others as equals is a keystone in learning how to be a friend.

As I talked with my senior editor at Thomas Nelson Publishers, Peter Gillquist, about the content, style, and direction of this book, he said, "I hope you'll tell stories about in-depth friendships the reader will long remember." I asked Peter for an example. Always the eager raconteur, Peter told me this moving story about his relationship with "Mr. Fred." It was such a beautiful account of a friendship that I've asked his permission to tell it here.

Mr. Fred had been brought up in Arkansas by his maternal grandparents, but as a young man he migrated to Texas and worked in a sawmill. Fred wasn't his real name. He adopted the alias after he had murdered a man in Texas in a barroom brawl. "The marshal told me to clear out of the state in twenty-four hours or face the death penalty," said Fred. So he fled the state of Texas and went to Grand Junction, Tennessee, with a young Mexican wife who left him a short time after they arrived. It seems nothing was easy about Mr. Fred's life.

Fred was jailed six or seven times after coming to Grand Junction, each time for his bootlegging activities. The townspeople said Fred's vocabulary was so foul that women with small children would cross the street and walk on the other side when they saw him coming toward them.

Until Fred's children reached their early teen years, they lived with him and their mother in a one-room house trailer that had no electricity or heat. Then they all left Mr. Fred to live by himself. That was when Peter met him.

Fred became a Christian because he was afraid of dying and going to hell. Having a purpose in life or being happy didn't interest him in the least. He just wanted out of hell and into heaven. The murder was his most awesome grief. Still, by the grace of God, he was able to join the likes of Moses and Paul on the celestial roll.

During the later years of Mr. Fred's life, his only family consisted of Peter, his wife, Marilyn, and their children. They fixed up an old storage house on some land they owned, laid a floor in it, insulated the walls and ceiling, put on a new roof, wired it for electricity, and put in a stove, refrigerator, electric heater, and fan. They would often have their friend over to the house for dinner, or they would take him a meal. Mr. Fred's stories about his childhood were endless and absolutely unforgettable.

It was late in November the year Peter took Mr. Fred to the hospital. He was seventy-nine. The last time they were together, Peter read him Revelation 21, all about the beautiful city of God. "I could listen to that all night," Mr. Fred whispered with a faint smile. Before the final good-byes were said, they clasped hands and prayed together. Peter knew he would never see Mr. Fred again this side of glory.

Then Peter told me, "Sometimes we'd just sit in our own rocking chairs by his stove for long stretches at a time and not say a word. When a friendship in Christ is established, it is on a level and depth beyond dependence upon mere words. It was because we did not *have* to talk to sustain our friendship that he was perhaps the easiest man I have known to be with. He became to me as a brother, nearly five decades removed."

Why do I tell this story? Because I wouldn't be a bit surprised if there is a "Mr. or Mrs. Fred" just waiting for you to be his or her friend. You'll never know until you get out there and try. Whether you "network" with a Mr. Fred or with a congregation or business client, treating others as equals should rate high on your list of priorities.

In his landmark book *Megatrends* author John Naisbitt gives us a primer for how we as human beings might best respond to the sophisticated technologies that will continue to assault us for the rest of the eighties. The book focuses on ten new directions that are already transforming our lives. I was especially fascinated by his chapter entitled "From Hierarchies to Networking," because his comments suggest a powerful relationship between this business trend to what is now becoming a new equality in friendships in the marketplace.

Naisbitt writes,

> The failure of hierarchies to solve society's problems forced people to talk to one another—and that was the beginning of networks....In a sense, we clustered together among the ruins of the tumbled-down pyramid to discuss what to do. We began talking to each other outside the hierarchical structure, although much of our previous communication had been channeled inside.
>
> As friends, as individuals, as members of small groups or large organizations, we exchanged resources, contacts, and information with the speed of a telephone call or a jet airplane ride, with the high touch of our own voices set against the din of a world swarming with too much data and too much knowledge.[2]

What Naisbitt and other "futurists" are telling us loudly and clearly is that we will all be working more closely with each other in the future than ever before. The strictly enforced pecking order is slowly becoming a thing of the past. While absolute equality will never exist, we must realize it is to our physical, social, and emotional benefit to truly regard and treat those around us as equals. Because just as the whole is greater than the sum of its parts, so are the thoughts, concerns, and well-conceived plans of an unthreatened few better than the isolated work of one.

This new arrangement will, I believe, also create the atmosphere for a rich harvest of new friends. Are all your friends just like you? Or have you opened your heart and mind to those who talk, think, and even act differently? Meet them. Get to know them and their families. Then be prepared to be surprised by the joy of fresh, new friendships.

My Friend the Buddist

He was once a commandant in the South Vietnamese marine corps. Later he was appointed chief of staff, and finally he assumed the post of governor of the province of Saigon. His name is Khang Lee.

Khang and his beautiful wife, Thu, had been good friends to me and to World Vision during the terrible war days in Vietnam, Laos, and Cambodia. This beautiful couple had a special appreciation for what we were trying to do to help alleviate the tremendous suffering of the Vietnamese people. As a result, they did everything they could to help us do our work effectively in that land. Khang was a devout Buddhist, but that did not prevent him and his wife from opening their home and their hearts to me over and over again.

It was finally clear that the South would not win the war. After seeing that hundreds of others were placed on airplanes or had secured other means of escape from Saigon, my friend Khang Lee boarded the very last helicopter on the roof of the American Embassy in Saigon. It was a sad, bitter farewell. To add to the pain, Khang had become separated from his wife, and he had no idea where she was.

However, we had a prearranged plan. If the two of them were in fact separated, they were both to contact me in the United States. We then lost contact. But one day I received a call. Khang had arrived in Camp Pendleton in California. He was safe, but he had no idea where his wife was. I said I was waiting for her call. Several days later she called me. She had been sent to a camp in Arkansas. To make a long story short, the two were reunited and World Vision sponsored them and helped them make adjustments to their new lives in the United States.

One day I was helping Khang buy a car when he turned to me and said, "Mr. Ted, I want to become a Christian. But I don't want to do it because you helped me. I will do it because I want Jesus to be in my life." While still in Vietnam, he had obtained a copy of a Christian book of biblical promises which had had an incredible impact on his life.

I couldn't hold back the tears. Even though it is not in his culture for a man to cry, he too got a bit misty. It was an incredible moment of friendship, and one neither of us will ever forget.

Some weeks later we got together after the evening church service at Lake Avenue Church in Pasadena. I had been thinking of Khang almost daily, and I'm convinced the

Holy Spirit was preparing both his heart and mine for what was about to happen.

As we sat in our home I said, "Khang, is it not time to consider inviting Jesus into your heart?" A smile crossed his face, his eyes flashed, and he said, "I'm so glad you said that. I *am* ready. Can I give my heart to Jesus right now?" I tell you, this big Swede and his slightly built Vietnamese friend hugged and prayed and gave thanks to God for His great mercy and love. The angels in heaven simply had to be singing in extra volume at that very moment as one more precious soul entered the kingdom.

Dorothy and I continue to see Khang and Thu. Their children have graduated from UCLA with honors, and they too have become committed followers of Jesus. I saw Khang just the other day, and he said, "I have such a purpose for living now, more than ever before. I hope you will always know I'm glad we are friends. I pray we may be friends forever."

We will!

Khang and I started out with seemingly nothing in common. He was a Vietnamese officer; I was with World Vision. He was Buddhist, and I was Christian. Our homes were thousands of miles apart. We spoke different languages, ate different foods, and espoused different world views. Nevertheless our mutual respect and willingness to accept each other as equals made all the difference. It provided the framework for us to become friends.

Five Guidelines for Treating Others as Equals

The famed doctor and humanitarian, Dr. Albert Schweitzer, was right when he said, "We are all so much together, but we are all dying of loneliness." Much of the reason for this is that too often we refuse to associate with other people in our community, our offices, even our churches. More often than not it takes a community disaster—a fire, a terrible accident, a flood, a violent snowstorm—for us to meet our neighbors.

With a minimum amount of effort, beginning right now, you and I can do something significant to enrich our own lives and the lives of others by making the conscious choice to reach out and treat others as equals.

1. *Recognize that the more you give away, the more you will receive.* It's a law of the universe, God's law. It's impossible to give your love away without its coming back to you ten, twenty, or even one hundred times over. I could write every single thing I know about the fine art of friendship, and when I'm through, I still have every idea, every insight, every thought I've given to you. When you improvise on what I've said, and when you put it through your own grid and give it back to me, then I become the richer for it.

Exercise: Beginning today, share yourself with a wonderful, *new* cross section of people. They are everywhere—school, next door, the beauty salon, the library, the office—and they are all potential friends. Your love and caring will be returned to you in ways you never imagined.

2. *Let people know your differences so they can see who you really are.* Just as no two snowflakes are alike, so no two people will ever be the same. Where did we ever get the wild idea that we have to be photocopies of each other to enjoy each other? If anything, that sort of relationship appears to be designed for boredom. When was the last time you made it a point to talk to someone you knew had a radically different point of view from yours? Were you able to listen? Really listen?

Exercise: Celebrate who you are, and thank a loving God who made you different from everyone else. Then look for ways to share that incredible uniqueness with others whether or not they are like you. It could change your life.

3. *Labels are killers.* Leo Buscaglia calls labels, "distancing phenomena." What is a lower economic family anyway? What is a black man? A white man? What is a Jew, a socialist, a Republican, an evangelical? I've never known two individuals identified in these ways who were exactly alike. Have you? These words are labels—nonthinking tags we slap on people we often feel have nothing to say to us. Unless we change our approach to persons right now we're going to lose out. Someone has wisely reminded us we didn't all come over in the same ship, but we're all in the same boat. It's true. Our similarities far surpass our differences.

Exercise: Every time you use a label as short cut language to talk down another human being, stop and think. Remember that labels are killers, and when you use them, you are damaging your opportunities for friendship.

4. *Refuse to merely exist. Live creatively.* If we only knew how great is our potential, if we only knew how we settle for so little, we would be absolutely miserable. Let's live life to the fullest. None of us is on this earth for very long. In fact it's a very short trip! So let's make today count! In so doing, let us leave a legacy of friendship that will be passed on to other generations. See the sun around you and within you, and then help make that same sun in others.

Exercise: Set aside a minimum of five minutes each day as your own personal friendship time. Talk to someone you've never talked to before. Be an encouragement. Never let a day go by without paying someone a compliment. Treat the waiter who refills your coffee cup as an equal. Say thank you for every act of kindness, no matter how small. An "excuse me" or "I'm sorry" will gladden the heart of everyone you come in contact with. These not-so-little acts of kindness will not only bring a spark of hope to the one who receives your warmth but will also remind you how much you need to be grateful for all those around you.

5. *Reactivate your childlike heart.* Jesus rebuked His disciples on one occasion because they didn't quite understand how much He loved children. He reminded them—and us—that heaven itself is made up of those who never lose their childlike spontaneity, their childlike heart that remains vulnerable, impressionable, and open to life. Unfortunately, if we're not careful, as we get older we get a hardening of the childlike arteries. We sometimes don't laugh as easily as we once did, and we get painfully serious. I guess we forget it's a lot more work to tense our muscles than to keep them relaxed. The truly great man or woman does not lose the spirit of the child's heart. If we can somehow recapture the freshness of that childlike spirit, we will find ourselves free to explore the most wonderful relationships, regardless of race, economic status, or creed.

Exercise: Consider inviting several people from a variety of ethnic backgrounds to your home. Ask each to sing, dance, play musical instruments, or recite stories and poems from "the old country." Expand your horizons. Get out of the rut of spending time only with familiar people. You might discover some more wonderful diamonds of friendships...right in your own back yard. Who knows what riches may await you!

Some stories are so good they bear repeating. Earl Nightingale tells one such tale in his marvelous audiocassette series, *Insight.* It's the story of a young man who chose to go the extra mile, only to discover that one single act of kindness changed his whole life.

On a stormy night many years ago, an elderly man and his wife entered the lobby of a small hotel in Philadelphia. The man helped his wife to a chair, then went to the desk. "All the big hotels in town are filled. Could you please give us a room here?"

The clerk explained that there were three conventions in town and no rooms to be had anywhere. "All our rooms are filled, too," he said. "Still, I can't send a nice couple like you out into the rain at one o'clock in the morning. Would you, perhaps, be willing to sleep in my room?"

The man replied that they couldn't put the clerk out of his own room, but the clerk insisted. "Don't worry about me. I'll make out just fine."

Next morning, as he paid his bill, the elderly man said to the clerk, "You're the kind of person who should be the boss of the best hotel in the country. Maybe, someday, I'll build one for you."

The clerk looked at the man and his wife and smiled. The three of them had a good laugh over the man's joke. Then the clerk helped them with their bags to the street.

Two years passed, and the clerk had forgotten the incident when he received a letter from the elderly man. It recalled the night of the storm, and enclosed was a round-trip ticket to New York.

When the clerk reached New York, the man led him to the corner of Fifth Avenue and 34th Street and pointed to a great, new building there, a palace of reddish stone with turrets and watchtowers, like a fairyland castle thrusting up into the sky.

"That," said the other man, "is the hotel I have just built for you to manage."

"You must be joking," the young man said, not quite know-ing whether or not to believe his host.

"I most assuredly am not joking," the older man said with a sly smile.

"Just who are you?"

"My name is William Waldorf Astor. We are naming the ho-tel the Waldorf-Astoria, and you are to be its first manager."

The young man's name was George C. Boldt. And that's the story of how he went from a small, nondescript hotel in Philadelphia to become manager of what was then one of the finest hotels in the world.[3]

Astor knew that Boldt's kindness had no thought of gain and thus came about a friendship that crossed all status and economic lines. The clerk—surely with only a modest in-come—chose to help a man who was a total stranger because the man had a real need. Little did he know he was giving his bedroom to one of the wealthiest men in the country. He could just as easily have been one more stranded business-man in Philadelphia that cold, stormy night.

Conversely, that seed of friendship, once planted, came back to the clerk in the form of great position and greater fi-nancial prosperity. I tell that story for one reason alone.

Whether the angels we attend are poor, wealthy, middle income, white, black, yellow, or brown, all that is required of us is that we extend a word, a deed of friendship. If we do it for personal gain, we will have already received our reward and that will be the end of it. But if we reach out unselfishly in compassion to those all around us, our hearts will be blessed forever.

It's the kind of thing that can and will happen to you when you begin to believe and embrace the principle of treating others as equals. You'll never know what angels you are attending until you begin to move beyond yourself. You'll discover it's a wonderful way to live.

I wouldn't be a bit surprised if a very special person is in your world just waiting for you to be his or her friend, and he or she may be much closer than you imagine. I think Yogi Berra of the Yankees organization said it best: "You can see a lot by just watching." After you've watched and taken the time to observe those around you who need a friend, then move to the next step. Act! Pay no attention to the world's foolish and manmade barriers. Step out in confidence among all those equals and be a friend.

7

If you think that praise is due him
Now's the time to slip it to him,
For he cannot read his tombstone
When he's dead.
—Berton Braley

PRAISE AND ENCOURAGEMENT

In our last chapter we noted that treating others as equals is a main ingredient in the fine art of friendship. Without that brick in building our house of friendship, the structure will easily fall on hard times. But that same house needs yet another building block—one we too easily forget.

My friend and colleague and the best-selling author, Dr. James Dobson, tells a powerful story in the opening chapter of his book *Hide or Seek* that I want to share with you. I guarantee once you read the account of this young man's life, it will be a story you'll never forget!

He began his life with all the classic handicaps and disadvantages. His mother was a powerfully built, dominating woman who found it difficult to love anyone. She had been married three times, and her second husband divorced her because she beat him up regularly. The father of the child I'm describing was her third husband; he died of a heart attack a few months before the child's birth. As a consequence, the mother had to work long hours from his earliest childhood.

She gave him no affection, no love, no discipline, and no training during those early years. She even forbade him to

90

call her at work. Other children had little to do with him, so he was alone most of the time. He was absolutely rejected from his earliest childhood. He was ugly and poor and untrained and unlovable. When he was thirteen years old a school psychologist commented that he probably didn't even know the meaning of the word "love." During adolescence, the girls would have nothing to do with him and he fought with the boys.

Despite a high IQ, he failed academically, and finally dropped out during his third year of high school. He thought he might find a new acceptance in the Marine Corps; they reportedly built men, and he wanted to be one. But his problems went with him. The other marines laughed at him and ridiculed him. He fought back, resisted authority, and was court-martialed and thrown out of the marines with an undesirable discharge. So there he was—a young man in his early twenties—absolutely friendless and shipwrecked. He was small and scrawny in stature. He had an adolescent squeak in his voice. He was balding. He had no talent, no skill, no sense of worthiness. He didn't even have a driver's license. Once again he thought he could run from his problems so he went to live in a foreign country. But he was rejected there too. Nothing had changed. While there, he married a girl who herself had been an illegitimate child and brought her back to America with him. Soon, she began to develop the same contempt for him that everyone else displayed. She bore him two children, but he never enjoyed the status and respect that a father should have. His marriage continued to crumble. His wife demanded more and more things that he could not provide. Instead of being his ally against the bitter world, as he hoped, she became his most vicious opponent. She could outfight him, and she learned to bully him. On one occasion, she locked him in the bathroom as punishment. Finally, she forced him to leave.

He tried to make it on his own, but he was terribly lonely.

After days of solitude, he went home and literally begged her to take him back. He surrendered all pride. He crawled. He accepted humiliation. He came on her terms. Despite his meager salary, he brought her seventy-eight dollars as a gift, asking her to take it and spend it any way she wished. But she laughed at him. She belittled his feeble attempts to supply the family's needs. She ridiculed his failure. She made fun of his sexual impotency in front of a friend who was there. At one point, he fell on his knees and wept bitterly, as the greater darkness of his private nightmare enveloped him.

Finally, in silence, he pleaded no more. No one wanted him. No one had ever wanted him. He was perhaps the most rejected man of our time. His ego lay shattered in fragmented dust! The next day, he was a strangely different man. He arose, went to the garage, and took down a rifle he had hidden there. He carried it with him to his newly acquired job at a book-storage building. And from a window on the third floor of that building, shortly after noon, November 22, 1963, he sent two shells crashing into the head of President John Fitzgerald Kennedy.[1]

Each time I read this brutal account of how Lee Harvey Oswald grew up friendless, without love, encouragement, praise, or discipline, a chill races down my spine. I'm reminded we often are guilty of treating people the same way, sometimes those we truly love most. Where we could have loved, we stubbornly withheld affection. When it would have been so easy to respond with a smile and a compliment, we criticized. When we were confronted with a mole hill, we turned it into an emotional Mount Everest. When a single word of encouragement would have won the day, for whatever dark reasons we chose to remain silent.

In so doing, we probably did not begin the psychic programming of a killer, although there is no guarantee of that.

We certainly did some killing of our own, because we aimed our rifle of rejection at that person's self-esteem and self-respect. We unloaded our shells; we called in the troops; we dropped the bomb; we won a little war.

Or did we? During that moment of unkindness part of our friend, our spouse, our colleague, our child died a little inside. However, what we perhaps failed to notice was that we died a little too. This is what happens to us when we fail to remember the seventh powerful principle of the fine art of friendship.

---

7. Be generous with legitimate praise and encouragement.

The Adventures of Memo Man!

Some members of my staff call me the "memo man." Others insist I'm hopelessly afflicted with memo madness and have fostered an organization-wide conspiracy that promotes memo mania. I'm told that words like *memo machine* and *management by memo* often hang over conversations where my name is mentioned. I cannot deny that the memo is for me what the seven-hundred-page novel is to James Michener.

I use memos to say a friendly hello, to say thank you, to encourage, to reprimand, to announce, to praise, and to express sincere appreciation. Most of my time at the dictaphone involves asking my secretaries and assistants to "take a memo." When all is said and done, I take all the ribbing about being "Mr. Memo" in the playful spirit in which it is intended.

On the day of her retirement, Dorothy Haskins, an employee of more than ten years, asked me to come down to her office. I did, not knowing what to expect. She reached over and picked up a gigantic book that was so heavy I had to help her lift it. It obviously held considerable value for Dorothy, because the book was beautifully bound. She asked mysteriously, "Well, what do you think this is?"

I said I didn't have the foggiest idea.

"Well, then," she went on, "let me show you." To my amazement, she leafed through page after page of every single one of the memos I had written her during her entire ten years at World Vision. I couldn't believe what I was seeing. They went on endlessly! At that moment I had to say to myself: *So that's what I've been doing with all my time!*

In Dorothy Haskins's case it was encouraging to note that most of the memos were of thanks, a compliment, or a word of encouragement. I don't say that in an attempt to ingratiate myself with you the reader. But I must say this. As I quickly scanned my ten years of dictation to Dorothy, I was truly grateful that God had given me the desire and, hopefully, the ability to be an encouragement to others. As I looked over that huge volume I felt good inside.

In fact, I was so moved by Dorothy's gesture that I could hardly wait to thank her in the manner to which she had become accustomed. Of course, I promptly thanked her with a memo!

The Old Swede Who Knew How to Love

It was Valentine's Day, 1984. Robert Larson, my friend and colleague who has been of such immeasurable help in researching and writing this book, was shaken awake by the telephone at 4:00 A.M. It was his mother in South San Francisco. Choking through her tears, she told Bob a team of paramedics had just arrived in the family living room, and at that very moment they were trying to save his dad's life. The seventy-four-year-old pastor and friend to so many lay pale and motionless on the floor, stricken by a massive heart attack. At 5:00 A.M. another call came. Bob's dad was dead.

For the next six days, Bob and his family were at Anna Larson's side, comforting, holding, and reminding her that Harry Larson had literally given his heart for the people he loved.

It had been my privilege to meet Dr. Larson on several occasions. I remember him as that "dear old Swede." He always had a kind word for everyone. He was an encourager and always a strong supporter of the work of World Vision and of missions throughout the world. For forty years he had touched the lives of the people of South San Francisco. For forty years he had loved and cared for them—and for some, in ways they had ever known.

When Bob returned to Los Angeles after the funeral, he told me some of the stories he heard after his dad's death. One man, weeping over the open casket, told Bob last Christmas he and his family had not received their social security checks. There was no money for food, the rent was due, and unpaid medical bills were stacking up. When Harry Larson heard about it, he bought several bags of groceries and took them to the home of his friends. He also gave them a generous check to help them along. He continued this week after week, until they were able to get back on their feet.

A former bank executive in town, a devout Roman Catholic, took Bob's hand after the service and said, "Your dad and I were so close. We'd meet downtown almost every day.

He'd ask me what I learned at Mass that morning, and he listened as I told him. Then he'd give me his sermon outlines for the next few Sundays, and I would listen. He was my dear friend. I'll miss him. He always had a good word for me. He was such an encouragement."

The stories went on and on about this man's friendships. His friendships truly lasted a lifetime, and he enjoyed relationships built on praise and seeing the good in others.

Why is it often so difficult for us to say an encouraging word to those we love the most? Why do we tend to overlook the obvious good and dwell instead on the negative? What are the reasons for the roadblocks we set up that keep us from truly being a friend to those we love the most? What can we do to change our attitudes and behavior?

Denis Waitley, in his magnificent book *Seeds of Greatness*, helps us address our dilemma on two specific fronts. I've found his insights especially helpful in handling conflicts both within my family and among my colleagues. Waitley suggests that "in communicating with others, always treat *behavior* and *performance* as being *distinctly separate* from the *personhood* or *character* of the individual you are trying to influence."

Here are some all-too-truthful communication examples from my own experience. Perhaps you will be able to identify with them!

Bad: "Why do you never meet your deadlines?"
Better: "When the work you're assigned isn't completed on time, it makes it difficult for many others involved in the project. Let's spend some time talking about it, OK?"

Bad: "How many times have I told you I expect
                 regular field reports from your department?"
Better: "I need more help in knowing what's going
                 on in your department, and I particularly
                 need *your* input. By the way, I'm getting
                 good feedback on your performance, and I
                 value your contribution."

Bad: "You're not telling me the truth!"
Better: "What you're telling me doesn't match up
                 with what I've heard. Let's check it out to-
                 gether."

The message? Criticize the performance, praise the per-
former—a top priority item in learning the art of friendship.
Every time I think or speak on the subject of encouragement and praise, a special poem comes to mind. Some people may consider it to be a bit corny. But I like it because its
verses capture the essence of what it means to be a friend.
Its message asks us to remember a great truth: *by denying
love and happiness to others we lose our own wished-for happiness.* Conversely, the more we share, the more we possess.
The more we praise and encourage, the greater the blessings
that flood our own souls. See if these lines speak to your
heart.

There are hermit souls that live withdrawn
In the peace of their self-content;
There are souls, like stars, that dwell apart,
In a fellowless firmament;
There are pioneer souls that blaze their paths
Where highways never ran—
But let me live by the side of the road

And be a friend to man.

Let me live in a house by the side of the road,
By the side of the highway of life,
The men who press with the ardor of hope,
The men who are faint with the strife.
But I turn not away from their smiles nor their tears—
Both parts of an infinite plan—
Let me live in my house by the side of the road
And be a friend to man.

I know there are brook-gladdened meadows ahead
And mountains of wearisome height;
And the road passes on through the long afternoon
And stretches away to the night.
But still I rejoice when the travelers rejoice,
And weep with the strangers that moan,
Nor live in my house by the side of the road
Like a man who dwells alone.

Let me live in my house by the side of the road
Where the race of men go by—
They are good, they are bad, they are weak, they are strong,
Wise, foolish—so am I.
Then why should I sit in the scorner's seat
Or hurl the cynic's ban?—
Let me live in my house by the side of the road
And be a friend to man.[2]

—"The House by the Side of the Road"
by Sam Walter Foss

What better time than now and what better person than
you to begin to become this kind of man or woman? Let
your friendship be genuine, your praise sincere, and your
encouragement generous to all you meet. Those whom you
touch with a word of kindness or deed of mercy—especially
your children—will long remember you, and they will thank
you for being a friend.

All of us who are parents have learned, more often than not the hard way, how much more is accomplished when we praise our children rather than constantly criticize them. Our three children, now each happily married to wonderful mates and each with their own families, were adopted as infants by Dorothy and me. We told them from their earliest childhood that we had selected them to join our family; they were our choice. Often, as little ones, we would hear them tell their playmates, "My Mom and Dad chose us; yours *had* to take you." We would always tell them how grateful we were for the delight and joy they were bringing to our lives and how proud we were of them. This closeness, praise, and appreciation have knit our family in a special way.

The three of them as adults have remained the closest of friends as well as brothers and sisters in Christ. It is also a source of great joy to Dorothy and me that they are our friends as adults as well as our sons and daughter.

Praising your child or grandchild costs you nothing, but what rich dividends it pays you in cementing relationships that endure the stress and difficulties of the years. Whether this encouragement is given to your children, your spouse, your neighbors, or the clerk at the local store, praise and encouragement will ultimately win the day. That is why spoken appreciation is so important in learning the art of friendship. Think about it. Do it!

NYACK COLLEGE MANHATTAN

8

*Give what you have. To some it may be
better than you dare to think.
—Henry Wadsworth Longfellow*

MAKING OTHERS NUMBER ONE

William Blake, the great eighteenth-century English poet, once wrote about the sensitive, vulnerable butterfly. If we grab at it as it sits on our shoulder and think solely of our own selfish interests to possess it, we snuff out its tiny, fragile life. On the other hand, when we relax, enjoy its brief company, and allow it to be its own important self, it lives and flourishes. Here are Blake's words:

> He who binds to himself a joy
> Does the winged life destroy,
> But he who kisses the joy as it flies
> Lives in eternity's sun rise

Blake's poetic sentiments remind me of what Martin Marty, theologian, writer, and critic, wrote in his book simply called *Friendship*, in which he says friendship, much like happiness, presents itself most readily when we don't seek it. Marty says, "There is no reason to make the search for friendship sound like an animal instinct. Friendship does not always come as a result of a search; it can come when we least look for it, just as it denies itself when we pursue it too earnestly and with pathetic eagerness."[1]

Friendship, then, can be just like the butterfly that lands on our shoulder. When it presents itself to us, we can seize it, smother it, and eventually kill it, or we can treat it with dignity, courtesy, and unfailing respect. That is why this eighth principle of the art of friendship is so important.

---

8. Make your friends Number One, preferring them above yourself.

You may be saying, "Hold on a minute. That is not usually what is written on that subject these days. We are being told over and over again to 'look out for Number One,' to take care of ourselves and our own self-interests—at any cost! We're reminded it's a jungle out there, where only the fittest survive and the winner takes all."

How do we reconcile these two strains of thought? Of course we need to take care of ourselves. I brush my own teeth, of course, put on my own socks, and tie my own shoelaces. Those are my responsibilities to myself. Yes, we do need to be our own best friend. In fact, until we're a true friend to ourselves we're not going to possess a great deal of self-worth, nor will we enjoy much of a relationship with others. (To say nothing of how little they are going to enjoy us.)

Of all the books and articles I've read on the critical subject of self-esteem, psychologist Dr. Neil C. Warren in his tremendously helpful book, *Make Anger Your Ally,* says it best. In a chapter entitled "And a Close Friendship with Yourself," he writes:

No friendship you have is as crucial to your self-esteem as that friendship you maintain with yourself. In fact, all your other friendships combined are not as important to the way you feel about yourself as your internal friendship with you is.

In support of this radical statement, consider the thousands of messages you send every day to your own self-assessment center. The content of these messages undoubtedly determines the way you evaluate your worth. And the evaluation you make of your worth invariably sets your self-esteem level.

After suggesting we list what we like about ourselves as part of an objective personal survey, Dr. Warren concludes,

But in the final analysis your appreciation of yourself will not depend on the length of your list of positive attributes. Rather, it will be due to your having been created unique and loveable. The fact is, that no one in history can replace you. And the clear word from the Bible is that you are enormously worthy solely on the basis of the magnificence of the created you.[2]

I'm glad my friend Dr. Warren wrote those words because they put the issue of "friendship with ourselves" in proper perspective. Once having established a friendship with ourselves, we can then, and then only, promote the good in others, look for ways to be genuinely complimentary, and be willing to take a back seat. After all, sitting in the back seat still gets us to our destination.

When you find yourself more concerned with *giving* friendship than in simply *receiving* it, you will discover you are in a most enviable position: You will be one who has tapped one of the richest mines of human relationships. You will have discovered the fine art of friendship.

Don't be like the man who said to the old potbelly stove, "Come on, give me some warmth and then I'll add the wood." It doesn't work that way for stoves *or* people *or* friendship.

One of the most moving books I've ever read is called *Letters to an Unborn Child,* written by David Ireland who, as he writes, is dying from a crippling neurological disease. David writes these letters to the unborn child still in the womb of his wife—a child he may never see. He will be unable to take his child to either ball games or ballet lessons. There will be no romps in the park, no stories read on daddy's knee. Still, he wants that child to know that dead or alive, "daddy loves his little boy or girl." Few stories express the selflessness of a woman for her husband, her lover, and her friend. Here are some of David Ireland's thoughts.

> Your mother is very special. Few men know what it's like to receive appreciation for taking their wives out to dinner when it entails what it does for us. It means that she has to dress me, shave me, brush my teeth, comb my hair; wheel me out of the house and down the steps, open the garage and put me in the car, take the pedals off the chair, stand me up, sit me in the seat of the car, twist me around so that I'm comfortable, fold the wheelchair, put it in the car, go around to the other side of the car, start it up, back it out, get out of the car, pull the garage door down, get back into the car, and drive off to the restaurant. And then, it starts all over again: she gets out of the car, unfolds the wheelchair, opens the door, spins me around, stands me up, seats me in the wheelchair, pushes the pedals out, closes and locks the car, wheels me into the restaurant, then takes the pedals off the wheelchair so I won't be uncomfortable. We sit down to have dinner, and she feeds me throughout the entire meal. And

when it's over she pays the bill, pushes the wheelchair out to the car again, and reverses the same routine. And when it's over—finished—with real warmth she'll say, "Honey, thank you for taking me out to dinner." I never quite know what to answer.[3]

What an account of tough love, energy, caring, and friendship! David's wife, Joyce, has to be the epitome of what it means to be willing to be Number Two, Three, Four, or whatever for the sake of her husband. I think it's good for us to hear about people like David and Joyce once in a while. It does something to us at our very core. And that is good! But how do you and I go about being Number Two and *liking* it?

My colleague, Ed Dayton, and I spend a large portion of our time giving time management seminars to pastors, teachers, leaders, and laypersons throughout the country. Because of our high profile in this subject and because we are so-called "experts," we are always being asked for our opinions, comments, and special insights.

After one exhausting session, I met privately for dinner with a small group of men who had been in the all-day conference. Because I had been the speaker all day, I had more or less assumed they wanted more "wisdom" from their leader.

Wrong! But it took me twenty minutes to realize it. I had continued to hold forth during the early part of dinner, taking the initiative, exercising leadership, motivating these fine men to do greater, more wonderful things, only to discover that was not what they wanted at this meal. Finally, one man said, "Ted, I think we have all had just about all the time management we can handle in one day. We just wanted to get together for fellowship." Don't make the mistakes I made.

1. *Catch the drift of the conversation before you assume people have assembled to hear what you have to say.* Consider the overwhelming words of 1 Corinthians 13. In the J. B. Phillips rendering of one of those powerful verses, we read, "Love has good manners and does not pursue selfish advantage." For the time being let's substitute the words *a friend* for *love*. Now it reads, "A friend has good manners and does not pursue selfish advantage." Wouldn't you agree?

I saw a sign on a colleague's wall recently that said: "Too many people operate on the assumption you don't need road manners if you're a fifteen-ton truck." Psychologically, if you must always draw attention to yourself, you have a problem. If you must receive all the praise and credit and are immobilized when you are not leading each and every conversation, then you don't know the first thing about how to be a friend. Psychologists refer to this malady as "performance anxiety." To counteract that problem, let's examine the next guideline.

2. *Learn to ask questions—and then wait for the answers.* A young woman in your office comes by your desk. She points to a letter in her hand and tearfully says, "My boyfriend has left with another girl. He's gone. Forever. He says he never wants to see me again." She breaks down and sobs some more.

If you are your own Number One, you might take her by the hand and say, "Now, now, that's not so bad. Let me tell you what happened to me, let's see was it two or three years ago? Yes, that's right, it was three years ago. You see, I was dating this guy who..."

What is the problem with this reaction? It says you are so

concerned with your own three-year-old problem that you cannot hear the pain of your friend now. What if, instead, you take her hand and say, "I don't know what to say. I'm so sorry. Are you going to be all right?" Then, "You probably don't need to cook dinner tonight. Why don't we go out together and get a bite. We can talk more then." Or, "What can I do to help you walk through this tough time?"

What a difference! *That* is a friend. *That* is being willing to stand in a Number Two position and feel good about it. Why? Because there are times in our lives when the concerns of another merit more attention than our own. It's one of the most important factors in learning the fine art of friendship.

Here is an exercise for you. Make it a point in the next day or two to talk with two or three friends. Tell them something wonderful that has happened to you, and note their response. Do they stay with you and your excitement? Or do they use the occasion to talk about themselves?

An even better experiment will be the next time someone turns to you and relates a situation—good or bad—that is on his or her mind. Will you ask questions that draw out how this person feels? Will you be patient in listening? Will you affirm your friendship by making your friend feel he or she is the most important person in the world at that moment? When you do, you'll be practicing one of the most powerful, yet rarely understood principles in learning how to be a friend. You'll find yourself in a perfect position to implement guideline number three.

3. *Take full responsibility for the pattern of growth you have experienced and encourage others to do the same.* The story is told of a trusted adviser of President Lincoln who recommended a candidate for the Lincoln cabinet. Lincoln de-

clined, and when he was asked why, he said, "I don't like the man's face."

"But the poor man is not responsible for his face," his adviser insisted.

"Every man over forty is responsible for his face," Lincoln replied, and the prospect was considered no more.

Just as you and I, according to Lincoln, are responsible for our "face," so are we responsible, with the patience and guidance of a loving God, for our own pattern of spiritual and emotional growth.

Dr. Wayne Dyer, lecturer and author of the best-selling book *The Sky's the Limit*, warns against our mindless conforming to the ideas and whims of the many influences that surround us. Dr. Dyer writes:

> In counseling I always think it is important to help anyone to resist automatic conformity to anything, because it detracts seriously from a person's basic human dignity by elevating other authority to a level higher than one's own. This is true for dominated children, wives, husbands, employees or anyone else: if you can't think for yourself, if you are unable to be other than conforming and submissive, then you are always going to be gullible, a slave to whatever any authority figure dictates.[4]

Those are good words to help us become our own persons, but they don't tell the whole story. In fact, there is great danger in becoming a law unto ourselves. The follower of Jesus has only one model, one standard, one mentor. If the gospel teaches anything, it teaches that the will of God for our lives is to be conformed, submissive, and molded into the image of His Son, Jesus Christ. Such a relationship is not slavery. It is ultimate freedom. It's the kind of 100 per cent allegiance that does not detract from our basic human dignity; instead, it's the one relationship above all others that makes you and me truly human. It is a friendship beyond comparison. Furthermore, it is a relationship worth sharing with others. The world around you is waiting to know that such a friendship is possible.

This verse has been underlined in my Bible as long as I can remember: "Seek ye first the kingdom of God, and his righteousness; and all these things shall be added unto you" (Matt. 6:33 KJV). What things? Things like joy, peace, hope, faith, courage, and love. It's all a matter of perspective, of remembering that the ultimate is Number One.

Too often the people who insist on being Number One do so at tremendous cost. It is always precarious to have to be on top all the time, and still more risky if perched there because of irrational thinking and careless behavior. Even a fallen Humpty Dumpty discovered the best of the king's horses and men didn't have all the answers when it came to putting him back together.

Look closely at your motivation for ascending the ladder. Take a hard look at your friendships. Do you really need to be Number One? I hope you will come to the conclusion that you don't need to worry about being any number at all.

It's my prayer that you'll discover something strangely wonderful beginning to happen to you when you work at taking full responsibility for your own pattern of growth and encourage others to do the same. Enjoy who you are. Enjoy your friends for who they are. Suddenly you'll find you will no longer be threatened by the success of others. You'll discover yourself able to compliment the one who has done well, won the award, made the touchdown, or been given the promotion.

You'll also find you will be able to be a better friend than ever before. You'll be able to appreciate without pressure to compete, applaud without wishing you were in the limelight. You'll notice you are relaxed, warm, and spontaneous in your praise, because you have chosen to conform to a higher power, One who has given you the strength and courage to be the friend He meant you to be. You can be Number 2, 22, or 222 and still enjoy it. The best news of all is that it's not idle theory. It works! It also puts you on firm footing for guideline number four.

4. *Mention your own faults before you begin criticizing your friend.* If you want a sure-fire way to keep from usurping the Number One position in a relationship, this is it. How can you feel superior when you choose to take the initiative in admitting a mistake or misguided action you've made? This doesn't mean you are inferior or ignorant, but it does put your friend on notice that you are honest about yourself. This attitude of honesty creates a fresh, convincing atmosphere of trust and camaraderie, qualities lasting friendships thrive on.

I recall one day on an overseas trip being brutally curt and short with a committee that had worked diligently and long in preparation for a meeting we were to conduct in that city. It was my responsibility to make certain everything would be in order, and upon my arrival, I found that practically all my instructions had been either ignored or wrongly executed. Frustrated, I verbally tore into those people who had worked so hard in their own cultural milieu, which I did not fully understand.

I had great difficulty sleeping that night. The next day I called them together to apologize. Gratefully, they accepted my apology and carried out their responsibilities in their *own* right, good way, and the event was wonderfully blessed of God. From that experience of vulnerability developed a warm friendship that has lasted over the years.

My problem was simple. I saw it as "my show," and I wanted it done my way. I wanted to be Number One. I wanted it done the American Way, the Red, White, and Blue Way, the way we do it at home! What a mistake! In spite of all my overseas experience, I had forgotten one of the most important principles of friendship. Be willing to stand back, and let your friends be Number One!

Someone has said that it is the weak who are cruel. Gentleness can only be expected from the strong. What a good word to motivate us to admit our errors. Learn to share them with a friend before you are critical of his or her actions. It adds to your stature to admit you are fully human.

5. *Do your part to make this planet a friend-ship.* One of my favorite verses of Scripture reads, "And outdo one another in showing affection." Just think what would happen if you and I engaged in that happy activity for even five minutes a day every day. The change in us and in our friends would be revolutionary. Besides, is it really so difficult to say something nice to those around you?

What about the waitress who in spite of being harried and rushed gives you exceptional service? Be a friend and tell her so. (And don't forget to leave a terrific tip!) What about the elderly woman who sits alone all day in the musty lobby of a retirement home with nothing to do and no one to care about her? Isn't there something you can do or be to demonstrate you care? If you regard yourself as Number One, chances are you'll just let her sit there growing old alone. But miracles begin to happen within you when your love exceeds your reach, when you make her and others Number One.

What about your children or your spouse? If you are going to learn how to be a friend, what better place to start than at home! You might be the father or the mother, but that doesn't mean you are a ruler whose divine right is to treat your family members as lesser servants. We all know how disparaging and unkind we can be to each other. Too often, we show the least amount of courtesy and friendship to the ones we say we love the most. We compliment the mailman, the milkman, our employees, and the people in the beauty salon, but we never compliment our own children, our own husband or wife. What a crime!

Don't let a day go by without seeing something good in your loved ones. Once you've seen it, then say something. Don't remain silent. Some days you might have to struggle a bit to find something, but you'll find it. When you do, don't be bashful. In a recent lecture, university professor Leo Buscaglia exhorted his listeners to do something about this: "I'm always telling teachers it's impossible for children to deal with a concept that out of fifty, they got forty-nine wrong. Why not tell them, 'Johnny, you got one right! Bravo! Tomorrow we're going to make it two!' "

He went on:

Remember what Grandma used to say, "You catch many more flies with honey than you do with vinegar." So why do we concentrate on the negative all the time—what you should be—what you should do? And all under the guise, "I'm telling this because I love you."...Those people whom we should be reinforcing the most because we love them so much are often the people we tell the least. And that's a pity. So in your home is where you begin to set this atmosphere of personal dignity. Telling people that they *are* beautiful.[5]

Buscaglia's words remind me of the the late, great football coach, Paul "Bear" Bryant. Several years ago, he was quoted as saying this about himself and his team:

I'm just a plowhand from Arkansas, but I have learned how to hold a team together. How to lift some men up, how to calm down others, until finally they've got one heartbeat together, a team. There's just three things I'd ever say:

If anything goes bad, I did it.
If anything goes semi-good, then we did it.
If anything goes real good, then you did it.

That's all it takes to get people to win football games for you.[6]

Not only football games. It's also the winning attitude that nourishes the kinds of friendships that last a lifetime. Bear Bryant worked at getting his team to function with "one heartbeat," and so it should, and can, be between us and our friends.

When you are willing to be Number Two or Three or Four or Five Hundred, you'll discover you possess an inexhaustible supply of love, compassion, and friendship to share with those around you. Whether or not you do this is completely up to you. It's your choice. Choose love, choose hope, choose caring, choose to believe in those around you. Look for the best in others. Make your friends Number One. It will revolutionize your world.

*The best exercise for the heart is to reach
down and pull other people up.*
—Anonymous

9

THE RIGHT MOTIVE

In the first eight chapters we've seen some of the key ingredients that go into the making of the fine art of friendship. Principle number one reminded us to work at developing those relationships in which we demand nothing in return. We then saw how it takes a conscious effort to nurture an authentic interest in others to create a meaningful friendship. Not surprisingly, principle number three called to our attention that we are all one-of-a-kind creatures and that it takes time, often a very long time, to truly understand and appreciate one another.

We saw the importance of the fourth principle of learning how and when to close our mouths and just listen to our friends. That was then the basis for principle number five which dealt with our "being there" with our friends at those special, unguarded, even raw moments of fear, joy, celebration, and sorrow.

The sixth principle of the fine art of friendship reminded us of what may be the most difficult area of all—treating others as equals. That key principle then led us to recognizing the vital importance of praise and encouragement in nourishing friendships. If we can do that, then we will come closer to following the eighth principle of making our friends Number One, preferring them above ourselves.

We now come to principle nine and ten. Without them our discourse on friendship would be woefully inadequate because they provide the motive for our pursuing and developing the fine art of friendship.

A gospel preacher, his spirits low, went into his sanctuary one morning to pray. As he fell to his knees he cried out, "Oh, Lord, I am nothing! I am nothing!"

The assistant minister happened to enter just at that moment. Overcome by the humility of the senior pastor, he too dropped to his knees. He began crying aloud, "Oh, Lord, I also am nothing, a mere nothing."

The janitor of the church, awed by the sight of the two men of God praying with such fervor, put his broom and dust pan aside and joined them, moaning, "Oh, Lord, I too am nothing. I am nothing at all."

At this, the assistant minister opened one eye, nudged the senior pastor, and whispered, "Now look who thinks he's nothing."

Motives! There are all kinds of them, and you and I possess them whether or not we're aware of their powerful influence on us. They're good and they're bad. Some motives—and these are the tricky ones—are neither good nor bad. Nevertheless, these sometimes blind forces within guide our lives, shape our friendships, and help determine our life's work.

For Vince Lombardi, the legendary coach of the Green Bay Packers, motive was the key issue in everything he said and did. Here is one brief but inspiring talk he made to his football team.

After the cheers have died and the stadium is empty, after

the headlines have been written and after you are back in the quiet of your own room and the Super Bowl ring has been placed on the dresser and all the pomp and fanfare has faded, the enduring things that are left are: the dedication to excellence, the dedication to victory, and the dedication to doing with our lives the very best we can to make the world a better place in which to live.

What a powerful statement of motive for all of us! Dedication to excellence, commitment to victory, passion to do our very best, to make this world a better place to live!

What a way to live! What a great way for us to think about our friendships! Just think what would happen if you and I were to take Lombardi's words to his team and apply them to our relationships. Why, we would never be the same again, nor would our friends. Life would take on a freshness and joy and pleasure that would change our lives. We'd soon discover that the fine art of friendship would, in practical terms, become the fine art of loving.

Here's what all too often happens. We start to become legends in our own minds. We begin believing our own press releases! We make it big (regardless of the true size of our world), and then we don't rest until everyone knows about our achievements. We find ourselves heaping great doses of harsh criticism onto the work of others. We work at convincing our colleagues their contributions are worth little or nothing. We exaggerate our own importance and develop an aura of implacable superiority. Very effective strategies—if we want to lose friends.

Another sure way to lose friends is to walk around with small but ever-present black clouds hovering over our heads. When someone asks us how we are, we say, "Well, I'm not feeling well, and the car wouldn't start this morning, and the kids are sick, and the boss didn't give me the raise he promised, and the dog chewed up my slippers, etc. etc., etc."

Of course it's always helpful if we're not dependable. For example, we won't bother to keep our word. We won't take our deadlines seriously. When a friend asks us to keep a trust, we'll say yes and mean no. We'll take his or her comments and introduce them into the gossip mill. We won't worry if our remarks destroy the character of another. We'll think only of ourselves and our own needs. We won't consider the quality of loyalty, and we'll regard others as people to walk over as we ascend our own ladder of success.

But who wants to behave in this manner? I don't. You don't. Why don't we eliminate all this negative, nonproductive activity as an ill-conceived idea? In a world that already has more than its share of anger, hatred, hunger, spiritual chaos, and domestic strife, you and I have a God-given mandate to be the healers, the lovers, not the haters. We are to be the counselors and consolers, not the combatants.

I know of no power, no force, or no more encouraging, relationship-healing, friendship-enhancing words in all of recorded literature than this ninth principle for friendship, a principle that believed and practiced will turn your world around. We talked in the last chapter about putting others before ourselves. In this chaper, we move to the next logical step.

---

9. **Learn to love God with all your heart, soul, mind, and strength. Then love your neighbor as yourself.**

For years, for some reason I could not come to grips with the full impact of that verse. I could understand loving God with all my energy and devotion. I was doing that every day. In fact, I was so highly motivated to serve my Lord that it took absolute priority in my life. I could also understand it was my Christian responsibility to love my neighbor. In fact, that wasn't really difficult at all. I enjoyed it. It was exciting to get close to my neighbors and see them one by one come to know the Lord.

The point I couldn't seem to grasp was in the last two words of the verse, "as yourself." I wasn't able to comprehend the goodness involved in loving myself. It just didn't seem right. To my mind it was selfish and ego-centered.

Then one day, while I was reading the late Reverend Cannon Samuel Shoemaker, the idea began to make sense. Shoemaker wrote, "When Christ commanded us to love our neighbors as ourselves He was commanding us to love ourselves. *If we will let ourselves be drawn back into God's love, we will find that we cannot go on hating that which God loves*" (italics mine).

In describing what he called "the eternal triangle," Dr. Shoemaker continued,

> We are beginning to learn from psychologists what religion has been telling us all along, that we are only "persons" as we are in relation to other persons. And the greatest other Person is God. So we are bound into a triangle, of God, other people, and ourselves....We easily see that we must have a relation to other people or to God; we do not so easily see that we also need a "relation" to ourselves...and the simple psychological fact is that, unless we are in good relation with ourselves, we shall not be in good relation with others, and we shall not be in good relation with God.[1]

Immediately the light began to dawn. I needed a right and proper sense of relationship to myself. Once I believed it and put it into practice, it made all the difference in the world.

I can't stress enough the importance of your recognizing your deep, intrinsic value. After all, God has created you and has invested of Himself in your very being. As a result you are of great beauty and of unique, indescribable worth. Because of this, you are to celebrate God's great love for you. You were also made for a purpose, and one of the great events for which God has prepared you is to share yourself with others in friendship.

Listen to the beloved apostle John. He lived his life to the fullest, and as an old man he penned these simple, profound words of what it means to love. In fact, in each of his three magnificent epistles, most of what he discussed concerned how to love.

> We know that we have crossed the frontier from death to life because we do love our brothers. The man without love for his brother is still living in death. The man who hates his brother is at heart a murderer, and you know that the eternal life of God cannot live in the heart of a murderer.

Then, to show how "love and life" are forever interconnected, John continued,

> We know what love is because Christ laid down his life for us. We must in turn lay down our lives for our brothers. But as for the well-to-do man who sees his brother in want but shuts his heart against him, how could anyone believe that the love of God lives in him? My children, let us love not merely in theory or in words—let us love in sincerity and in practice! (1 John 3:14–18 PHILLIPS)

Love is a word expressed in a thousand ways. From the sick, sordid, carnal "love" of X-rated movies to the love of a mother for her child. From the love of a God who sent His Son to give us life to the love of a husband for his wife or a wife for her husband. *Love* is the word songs and poems are made of; yet putting it into practice is often difficult for us to do. Still, it's true: "Love in your heart wasn't put there to stay. Love isn't love 'til you give it away."

When we begin to understand our need to love, and when we discover that to love is the only way to be in harmony with what God created us to be, then we create the environment that prepares us for the joy that comes with learning the fine art of friendship. For me that "environment" presented itself at thirty-five thousand feet.

In the more than three decades I have spent in my work with Christian agencies, I have had the privilege of traveling tens of thousands of miles to every continent, visiting over one hundred twenty-five nations in probably one hundred fifty or more separate trips. That is a lot of hours in the air sitting next to strangers.

Often the conversation with my seat-mate leads to questions such as, "What is your work?" "Where are you heading—and why?" "What is World Vision anyway—some international optical firm?"

Time and again, the conversation naturally turns to my witness of faith in my dearest friend, the Lord Jesus Christ. It is always a privilege to be able to give away my faith and share with another the greatest friend who ever lived. Even though I shouldn't be surprised anymore, I'm still somehow repeatedly amazed at how open and eager some fellow passengers are to pursue this subject. Other times the person next to me does not choose to discuss the matter further.

On occasion I have found a fellow believer, and that fellowship is always especially meaningful. Then there was the man in seat 14-A.

I was on my way to a conference in Egypt when I soon realized I was to be seated for twelve hours next to the great-grandson of one of my heroes, a former United States president. I was fascinated as he shared with me so many intriguing and little-known facts about this great American chief executive. During our long conversation I had the privilege to relate to him the truth of the resurrection and the magnificent hope the believer in Christ possesses.

"I'd give anything if I could believe, as you do, in an afterlife," he said. "But I just can't do it. Perhaps, one day I will."

It is my prayer that he will one day be joined to Christ and His church.

A few days later, on a return flight from Europe, the cabin was sparsely populated and I had the opportunity to speak at great length with one of the hostesses. I talked with her about the Christian life and all its richness and fullness. Rarely have I met one more open to the good news. I have no greater joy than to be motivated by God's great love for me, Ted Engstrom, and then share that love with friends new and old.

In preparing my thoughts for this chapter, I went through one of my sermon files and rediscovered what some of our greatest writers have written about this capacity for love and caring.

The famous early nineteenth-century preacher, Henry Ward Beecher, said, "No one can deal with the hearts of men unless he has the sympathy which is given by love ...you must have enough benevolence, not only for yourself, but for others, to pervade and fill them. This is what is meant by living a godly life."

Victor Hugo, French poet, dramatist, and novelist, wrote, "The greatest happiness of life is the conviction that we are loved, loved for ourselves, or rather loved in spite of ourselves."

The prolific American writer, Longfellow, declared: "Nor father or mother has loved you as God has, for it was that you might be happy when He gave His only Son. When He bowed His head in the death hour, love solemnized its triumph; the sacrifice there was completed."

Then I was reminded of these ever-so-sane words once discovered on an asylum wall:

> Could we with ink the oceans fill
> And were the skies of parchment made
> And every stalk on earth a quill
> And every man a scribe by trade,
> To write the love of God above
> Would drain the oceans dry,
> Nor could that scroll contain the whole
> Though stretched from sky to sky.

What powerful thoughts for living! What magnificent words and concepts to give us the courage to keep reaching out, to keep touching, caring, giving, and forgiving those around us! What encouraging words these are to help us keep loving and learning how to be a friend!

What is the fundamental reason we should love our neighbor? The answer can be found in John 16:27: "For the Father Himself loves you." How wide is that compassion? The Lord said, "I have loved you with an everlasting love" (Jer. 31:3). What about fickle friends? "A friend loves at all times" (Prov. 17:17), and "Many waters cannot quench love" (Song of Sol. 8:7). And forgiveness? First Peter 4:8 says, "Love will cover a multitude of sins."

What about the risks of friendship? Jesus said, "Greater love has no one than this, than to lay down one's life for his friends. You are My friends if you do whatever I command you" (John 15:13–14). Part of the good news of this message from our Lord is that it is never a harsh order from an unfriendly commander.

Like each of God's commandments to His people, this one is meant to inspire us to action and discipline, to carry out God's plan for our lives. To be a true friend takes time, energy, patience, courage, and determination to draw out the best in another in spite of the setbacks and discouragements.

One of my favorite stories is the old tale about the devil's clearance sale. The fable begins with Satan standing before a large table of tools on which were placed the sword of jealousy, the knife of fear, and the hangman's noose of hatred. Just about every tool in Satan's possession was for sale, and for a very high price.

Standing alone on an ornately carved wooden pedestal was a worn and battered wedge. It had obviously been used more than all the other tools put together. This wedge was the devil's most prized possession. It was the wedge of division between God's people. It was the only tool Satan needed to stay in business, and it wasn't for sale.

Why? Because he knew it was the most effective tool of the lot. You and I know it too. New and old friends will disappoint us. We will become discouraged in our attempts to be a friend. But a loving, understanding Father is always waiting to take our disappointments and turn them back into friendships.

Lasting friendships take persistence and constant effort, but they demand more than physical strength. The prophet Isaiah reminds us where the power for loving really comes from: "But those who wait on the LORD/Shall renew their strength;/They shall mount up with wings like eagles,/They shall run and not be weary,/They shall walk and not faint" (40:31). With that encouragement we will be granted the power to love our neighbors. We will once again rise up, confident, and be a friend. It is also what we need for loving our "enemies."

Surely one of the most remarkable men of this century is a man I'm privileged to call my cherished friend. He is Ugandan Bishop Festo Kivengere, resident of a country that took the unbridled anger and fury of the half-crazed, self-appointed president for life, Idi Amin.

For eight long years blood flowed from the innocent bodies of men, women, and children. Amin was no respecter of persons. A classic example of a paranoiac, he saw the enemy behind every tree, and each threat to him—imagined or real—was disposed of in the most horrible fashion imaginable.

Amin's infamous "State Research Bureau" kept tabs on these "enemies," and through its sophisticated underground network it was able to kill, maim, and destroy large numbers of Uganda's best and brightest. He used every means possible to perpetuate his power and his crimes.

During Uganda's darkest hours, our World Vision teams interviewed grieving families. We would hear stories of how five to six family members had been picked up in the dead of night, thrown into the trunks of cars, and taken out and shot. After we had heard literally hundreds of these stories it was difficult to separate truth from what might have been fiction, because there came a point where they were one and the same.

During this Ugandan holocaust if any one man had cause for anger and retribution, it was Anglican Bishop Festo Kivengere. His archbishop was ambushed and killed by Amin's troops. Festo's flock of faithful, Spirit-filled men, women, and children were gunned down, knifed, butchered, or raped. Yet, by the mercy of God, Festo was ultimately able to say, "I love Idi Amin." He wrote a book with that title, and in one section he declared:

> Peace is not automatic. It is a gift of the grace of God. It always comes when hearts are exposed to the love of Christ. But this always costs something. For the love of Christ was demonstrated through suffering, and those who experience that love can never put it into practice without some cost.
>
> I had to face my own attitude towards President Amin and his agents. The Holy Spirit showed me that I was getting hard in my spirit, and that my hardness and bitterness toward those who were persecuting us could only bring spiritual loss. This would take away my ability to communicate the love of God, which is the essence of my ministry and testimony.
>
> So I had to ask for forgiveness from the Lord, and for grace to love President Amin more, because these events had shaken my loving relationship with all those people. He gave assurance of forgiveness on Good Friday, when I was one of the congregation that sat for three hours in All Souls' Church in London, meditating on the redeeming love of Jesus Christ. Right there the Lord healed me, and I hurried to tell Mera [Festo's wife] about it. This was fresh air for my

tired soul. I knew I had seen the Lord and been released: love filled my heart.[2]

No sheer power of the will could have fostered such an attitude of love. No broad, humanistic appreciation of people could have produced the quiet strength and solid resolve Festo felt in his very bones for Idi Amin. This love for his neighbor, cruel and contemptible though he was, could only have come about as a result of a relationship with the living God. While Festo Kivengere and Idi Amin never again met, Festo continues to pray for the man who did his best to destroy the country that was once called the "gem of Africa." Festo remains willing and able to be Idi Amin's friend.

You and I are not likely to be placed in such a life-threatening position. Yet that same power of love manifested by Festo is available to you and me at this very moment. When you have a need to make restitution to your spouse, one of your children, a neighbor, perhaps a friend at church or in the office, start by remembering that "all power is given unto you." God has generously provided you and me with all the strength we'll ever need to be loved and to love. "Ask, and it will be given to you; seek, and you will find; knock, and it will be opened to you" (Matt. 7:7). What greater promise could you or I ever want? Yet, so much of the world system runs contrary to the essence of Christian truth. That's why what I call these "wonderful surprises" are so important to keep in mind as we reach out in love to our neighbors.

- The world says to despise your enemies. God's kingdom says to love those who hate you.
- The world tells you to strike back, get revenge, stay

mad, better yet—get even. The kingdom of God says to do good to those who mistreat you and wish you evil.

- The world says to fight to be Number One, climb to the top at any cost, step over people to get what you want. God's kingdom insists you must lose your life in service to others in order to truly find it.
- The world says the young, the tanned, and the beautiful are the ones who are going to make it. The kingdom serves notice that even a grain of wheat must go into the ground and die before it can live.
- The world says true riches are found in stocks and bonds, mutual funds, gas and oil investments, and shiny, expensive cars. The kingdom of God says only those intangible treasures stored in heaven have any ultimate value.
- The world says to take advantage of the masses, give the tax breaks to the rich, and exploit those who cannot fend for themselves. The kingdom makes it clear you are to befriend the poor, the sick, the widows, and the orphans.

What a contrast in values! What powerful motives! What a marvelous source of power becomes available to us when these kingdom principles are put into practice in our daily lives! It's a constant reminder we all need as we learn *the fine art of friendship.*

The only gift is a portion of thyself.
—Ralph Waldo Emerson

10

PROPER INTRODUCTIONS

Everything about the place says "end of the line." Yet, those thick, impenetrable walls of the seemingly inhospitable La Mesa Penitentiary in Tijuana, Mexico, house one solitary figure who never committed a murder, was never guilty of aggravated assault, burglarized no one's property, and at no time engaged in illegal trafficking of drugs.

Nonetheless, this person takes three meals a day with the men in the prison mess hall, sleeps in a cell, and is awakened each morning by the call of the penitentiary guard. Her name is Sister Antonia Brenner, a fifty-six-year-old California woman who insists, "This is not a job for me. It is my calling. The prison is my convent."

The inmates of La Mesa call her "The White Angel." Sister Antonia calls herself a "prisoner of love." If an inmate's mother or father is ill, Sister Antonia leaves the prison to pay a visit. When a prisoner's relative dies, Sister Antonia attends the funeral. When any of the one thousand semipermanent residents at La Mesa need a comb, a toothbrush, a lawyer, or just a friend, they know Sister Antonia is only a few cells away.

Much of what Sister Antonia does flies in the face of what

127

is taught in conventional penology texts. She will affectionately pinch the cheeks of prisoners, hold their hands, and
warmly hug them. Her attire obviously reminds everyone
whom she is there to represent. As you might expect, some
people consider Sister Antonia's unorthodox approaches to
rehabilitation both naive and dangerous. But such criticism
does little to deter this special "prisoner" from committing
herself even more deeply to the lives of the inmates.

On one occasion when she was being criticized for her un-
conventional methods, Sister Antonia took out a white napkin. Drawing a black dot in the middle, she asked, "What
do you see? You don't see the white of the napkin. All you
see is the dot. With the men here, most outsiders see only
that they are murderers or thieves. They don't see the rest of
them. I do. Yes, I see the bad in people, but I also see the
good."[1]

If you were to take a poll among the prisoners of La Mesa
Penitentiary, asking them for their definition of a friend,
you would get one overwhelming response—Sister Antonia!
She is the living example of our last principle of building
friendship.

---

10. Emphasize the strengths and virtues of others, not their sins and weaknesses.

To illustrate this principle, here's a story a friend of mine
told me recently. It seemed that Joe had just about had it
with his wife of three years. He no longer thought of her as
attractive or interesting; he considered her to be a poor
housekeeper who was overweight, someone he no longer

wanted to live with. Joe was so upset that he finally decided on divorce. But before he served her the papers, he made an appointment with a psychologist with the specific purpose of finding out how to make life as difficult as possible for his wife.

The psychologist listened to Joe's story and then gave this advice, "Well, Joe, I think I've got the perfect solution for you. Here's what I want you to do. Starting tonight when you get home, I want you to start treating your wife as if she were a goddess. That's right, a goddess. I want you to change your attitude toward her 180 degrees. Start doing everything in your power to please her. Listen intently to her when she talks about her problems, help around the house, take her out to dinner on weekends. I want you to literally pretend that she's a goddess. Then, after two months of this wonderful behavior, just pack your bags and leave her. That should get to her!"

Joe thought it was a tremendous idea. That night he started treating his wife as if she were a goddess. He couldn't wait to do things for her. He brought her breakfast in bed and had flowers delivered to her for no apparent reason. Within three weeks the two of them had gone on two romantic weekend vacations. They read books to each other at night, and Joe listened to her as never before. It was incredible what Joe was doing for his wife. He kept it up for the full two months. After the allotted time, the psychologist gave Joe a call at work.

"Joe," he asked, "how's it going? Did you file for divorce? Are you a happy bachelor once again?"

"Divorce?" asked Joe in dismay. "Are you kidding? I'm married to a goddess. I've never been happier in my life. I'd never leave my wife in a million years. In fact, I'm discovering new, wonderful things about her every single day. Divorce? Not on your life."

What made the difference? Joe ultimately discovered that a new relationship with his wife was not something that would somehow appear out of the blue. He learned it was something he had to do. It all began to come together when *he* changed his attitude, when he started emphasizing the strengths and virtues of his wife, not her sins and weaknesses. The amazing thing is that Joe had no idea this would happen. He thought he was going to "stick it to her." Instead, they once again fell madly in love.

The same principle applies to friendship. Look around you, and it won't be difficult to focus on the bad and the ugly in others. That doesn't take much talent. Now take another look. Do you see anything good about them and their personalities? If there are people without a smile, give them one of yours. If an acquaintance is negative and always walks around with a little gray cloud overhead, point out something positive about that person. Recognize him or her as someone important.

How to Take the First Step

In a short story by French author Antoine de Saint-Exupery, a man writes these words to his friend:

> I am grateful to you for accepting me as you find me. What do I want with a friend who judges me? If I welcome a friend to a meal, I ask him to sit down if he limps, and do not ask him to dance.

> My friend, I need you as one needs a height on which to breathe![2]

I hope you see how important it is for you and me to be that kind of friend.

Over the years of our marriage, Dorothy and I have tried to make sure our home always had an "open door" to neighbors and friends. We haven't preached or lectured to these good friends. In fact, most of the time we've just carried on low-key discussions about children and grandchildren, ethics in business, our relationships with our spouses, and other subjects that are a constant concern to us all.

We called it "friendship evangelism"; we are genuinely interested in what is happening in the lives of our friends. These warm, positive times together underline the good and the positive in our neighbors and their families. Not surprisingly, these times together have made for an incredibly happy, fulfilled life for Dorothy, for me, and for our scores of friends. It's really true. You are allowed to keep only that which you consciously give away. Give away your friendship, and you will receive friendship in return. Give away your self, and your "better" self will return to you many times over. Accentuate the positive, share warmth and honest concern for those around you, and you'll be amazed at what happens. I recently heard a story of two different approaches by two literary groups at the University of Wisconsin. This story alone is proof enough of the power of focusing on the good in others.

Years ago there was a group of brilliant young men at the University of Wisconsin who seemed to have amazing creative literary talent. They were would-be poets, novelists, and essayists. They were extraordinary in their ability to put the English language to its best use. These promising young men met regularly to read and critique each other's work. And critique it they did!

These men were merciless with one another. They dissected the most minute literary expression into a hundred pieces. They were heartless, tough, even mean in their criticism. The sessions became such arenas of literary criticism that the members of this exclusive club called themselves the "Stranglers."

Not to be outdone, the women of literary talent in the university determined to start a club of their own, one comparable to the Stranglers. They called themselves the "Wranglers." They, too, read their works to one another. But there was one great difference. The criticism was much softer, more positive, more encouraging. Sometimes there was almost no criticism at all. Every effort, even the most feeble one, was encouraged.

Twenty years later an alumnus of the university was doing an exhaustive study of his classmates' careers when he noticed a vast difference in the literary accomplishments of the Stranglers as opposed to the Wranglers. Of all the bright young men in the Stranglers, not one had made a significant literary accomplishment of any kind. From the Wranglers had come six or more successful writers, some of national renown such as Marjorie Kinnan Rawlings who wrote *The Yearling*.

Talent between the two? Probably the same. Level of education? Not much difference. But the Stranglers strangled, while the Wranglers were determined to give each other a lift. The Stranglers promoted an atmosphere of contention and self-doubt. The Wranglers highlighted the best, not the worst.

Are you a strangler or a wrangler? Are you one who helps to bring out the best in your friends, or do you focus on the weaknesses of those around you? We all need to be properly critiqued from time to time, but no one needs a steady diet of criticism. Not our children, not our spouses, not our pastors, not our bosses or our employees. That's why our tenth principle is so vital: Keep emphasizing the strengths and virtues of others, not their sins and weaknesses. This may be the most important ingredient of all in learning the fine art of friendship.

God is ready to give you some fantastic opportunities to touch the lives of men and women closest to you, starting right now. In fact, those opportunities are staring you in the face at this very moment. It's your turn to act.

There's no question about it. We each have within ourselves the God-given ability to be a friend. However, the more we concentrate on stressing the weaknesses and inabilities of others, on fulfilling our own desires, and on achieving our own private happiness, the more frustrated, unhappy, and depressed we will become. But it's a different story when we begin looking for ways—and I mean *aggressively* looking for ways—of discovering the good in our friends. Perhaps the story of fifty-year-old Sammy will explain what I mean.

Walter, a close friend, takes considerable pride in the fact that he works out at his local athletic club one hour every day. The minute he gets off work, he is in his car and on his way to the local fitness center to subject his body to all sorts of punishment: weights, stationary bicycle, hydrafitness machines—the works.

One day there was a new man working out at the center. Walter didn't talk to him, but he saw "Sammy" stenciled on his gray sweatshirt, so he figured that was his name. Sammy seemed to be slow and lethargic, and he was nowhere near the pace of Walter's workout. Walter went through his routine without giving Sammy any further thought.

An hour later Walter was heading for the sauna to relax his tired, overworked muscles. But he had to wait a moment at the door to the sauna because Sammy was having trouble with the handle. Sammy finally opened the door and went inside. Walter sat across from him.

Walter looked at his sweating companion, but all he got was a vacant stare encased in a masklike face. Sammy slowly brought the towel to his forehead to remove some perspiration and then dropped the towel to his side.

Walter, normally a sensitive person, grunted to himself that old Sammy really didn't have much going for him. On top of that, Sammy even smelled funny. Walter was so turned off by Sammy's presence that he stayed in the sauna only half his normal time. Walter left without saying anything, showered, and went home.

The next day, the same thing happened. Sammy was there again. He was just as slow, his expression was no less masklike, and he still smelled just as bad. This time, Walter said something he later wished he'd left unsaid. I'll try to recreate the conversation as Walter told it to me:

Walter:	"What's your problem, old-timer?"
Sammy:	(*silence coupled with long, vacant stare*)
Walter:	"I said, 'What's going on?' I mean you come to the center to work out and you hardly move your body."
Sammy:	"I...I'm sorry...don't move so well anymore. The doctors are doing all they can to help, but not much hope. Yesterday, couldn't walk. Today, got a loud hum in my ears. Hurts."

Walter:	"Oh, I'm sorry. *(more compassionately)* What's the problem?"
Sammy:	"Parkinson's disease. Got tremors, especially in my fingers and hands. Not much feeling. It's rough. Too rare a disease to warrant much research money, I guess. So I just live with it. Sorry I've been a bother to you. Really sorry."
Walter:	"I...I don't know what to say, except I'm sorry for what I said. I hope you'll forgive me, Sammy."
Sammy:	"Oh, it's OK. Lots of people feel that way about me. It's just that I can't move any faster. I'm lucky to be able to even walk into this place. Lucky I'm alive."

That is not where this story ends. Day after day Walter and Sammy would meet. The days turned into weeks, then months. The two of them got to know each other well and in the process became close friends.

Then one day, Sammy didn't appear at the gym. Walter didn't think much of it at first, but Sammy wasn't there the next day or the next. He called Sammy's home only to discover that Sammy had died in his sleep a few nights earlier. Walter was told that Sammy was finally out of his misery, but that in his final hours he had told his wife, "Be sure you say good-bye to Walter. He was one of the best friends I ever had." Walter sat in my office and told me how he cried himself to sleep that night. He said he vowed never again to focus on the weaknesses of another. Walter had discovered one of the key ingredients to the fine art of friendship: emphasize that which is good in a friend. Walter will never be the same as a result of that experience with Sammy. Neither will I. Perhaps, neither will you.

Deciding to Change

As I was putting the finishing touches on the preparation of this book, I came across a marvelous story about a scientific experiment carried out by French entomologist, Jean Henri Fabre. It's a story about processionary caterpillars—wormlike creatures that travel in long, undulating lines, at the same cadence, same pace, with virtually no thought given to their ultimate destination. They simply play "follow the leader."

For the purpose of the experiment, Fabre coaxed a group of these caterpillars onto the thin edge of a large flowerpot so that the leader of the group was nose to tail with the last caterpillar in the slow, deliberate, nonending procession. It was impossible to determine who was leading and who was following.

Out of sheer habit and instinct, the ring of caterpillars circled the flowerpot for seven days and seven nights, until they finally began to die one by one, victims of starvation and exhaustion. All the while, a large supply of the food they liked best was close at hand, and plainly visible, but it was slightly out of range of the path so carefully trod on the top of the flowerpot. What a message for you and me!

That kind of thing can happen—and often does—when any person, group, philosophy, or idea is followed blindly. That is how habits become entrenched. It can happen as easily with people as it does with caterpillars. If your pattern of life has been not to reach out in friendship to others, let me warn you: It's tough to change. It takes courage and perhaps even the swallowing of some pride to step out and make a decision, to determine to embark on an exciting new course of being a friend. Still, I'm going to issue you this challenge.

If you relish being a private person, one who has refrained from making friends, I am going to ask you to step out of the line, so to speak, of your habit of isolation, get off the rim of the flowerpot—a rim that takes you nowhere—and *decide* to make friends.

Start today to

1. Develop the kinds of friendships in which you demand nothing in return.

2. Make a deliberate, conscious effort to nurture an authentic interest in others.

3. Celebrate the excitement that each of us is a one-of-a-kind creation and that it will always take time, often a long time, to understand one another.

4. Commit yourself as never before to learning how to listen.

5. Above all, when your friend needs you, simply be there, whether or not you know what to do or say.

6. Treat others as equals.

7. Work at being generous with legitimate praise and encouragement.

8. Make your friends Number One, preferring them above yourself.

9. Love God with all your heart, soul, and strength. Then love your neighbor as yourself.

10. Above all, emphasize the strengths and virtues of others, not their sins and weaknesses.

If you want to start living, if you want to discover the meaning of a rich, abundant, happy, successful life filled with friendships nurtured to last a lifetime, take these vital principles to heart and start making them work for you today. You'll find amazing things will happen when you take the initiative to give those around you the gift of yourself, when you make the conscious, loving effort to step out and learn *the fine art of friendship*.

AFTERWORD

For more than ten years Ted Engstrom has been my friend. He has encouraged me, loved me, listened to me, and walked with me through my good and bad times. He has always been available, courteous, polite, understanding, and affirming. Yes, I too get my share of those wonderful memos.

For me, Ted Engstrom is a valued personal treasure and faithful friend. Few men on earth, with the exception of my own father, have made such a permanent mark for good on my life. How can I be anything but eternally grateful to my friend, Ted Engstrom!

I thought I had lots of friends, and I do! But Ted Engstrom has hundreds. Literally. I know, because I talked to scores of them as I helped prepare the material for this book.

Thank you, Ted, for the privilege of working with you once again. Thank you, Ted, for personally living out the principles of friendship we've written about in these pages. Thank you, Ted, for being such a model of friendship to me and to thousands of others all across this world. Thank you, Ted, for teaching me so much about *the fine art of friendship*.

Robert C. Larson
La Canada, California

NOTES

Chapter 1
1. "Why a Good Friend is Hard to Find," *U. S. News and World Report*, September 26, 1983, 71–72.

Chapter 2
1. *Bits and Pieces*, December 1983, 21.
2. Judson Swihart, *How Do You Say "I Love You"?* (Downers Grove, Ill.: Inter-Varsity Press, 1977), 46–47.

Chapter 3
1. From "Getting to Know You," *The King and I*, by Richard Rodgers and Oscar Hammerstein II (New York: Williamson Music Co.).
2. Martin Buber, *Tales of the Hasidim: The Early Masters* (New York: Schocken Books, 1948), 11.
3. *Christopher News Notes* No. 265 (12 East 48th St., New York, N. Y. 10017).

Chapter 4

1. John Drakeford, *The Awesome Power of The Listening Ear* (Waco, Tex.: Word Books, 1967), 15.
2. Beth Day, "Standing Room Only for Silence," *Reader's Digest*, June 1958, 187–91.
3. H. Norman Wright, *More Communication Keys to Your Marriage* (Ventura, Calif.: Regal Books, 1983), 79–80.
4. Kenny Moore, "She Runs and We Are Lifted," *Sports Illustrated*, December 26, 1983–January 2, 1984, 38.

Chapter 5

1. *Insight* (Chicago: Nightingale-Conant Corporation, 1983).
2. Malcolm Muggeridge, *Something Beautiful for God* (New York: Ballantine Books, 1971), 55.
3. Ibid., p. 58.
4. Harold Wilke, "How to Unlock Your Limitations," *Guideposts*, November 1982, 16–17.
5. From *Saturday Evening Post*, May 28, 1949, 72.

Chapter 6

1. *Guideposts*, January 1984, 2–5.
2. John Naisbitt, *Megatrends* (New York: Warner Books, 1982), 191, 198–99.
3. "The Way Up," *Insight*.

Chapter 7

1. James Dobson, *Hide or Seek* (Old Tappan, N.J.: Fleming H. Revell, 1974), 9–10.
2. Taken from *Dreams in Homespun* (New York: Lothrop, Lee, and Shepherd Co., n.d.).

Chapter 8

1. Martin E. Marty, *Friendship* (Allen, Tex.: Argus Communications, 1980), 49–50.

2. Neil Clark Warren, *Make Anger Your Ally* (New York: Doubleday, 1983), 145–46.

3. David Ireland with Louis Tharp, Jr., *Letters to an Unborn Child* (New York: Harper & Row, 1974), 33–34.

4. Wayne Dyer, *The Sky's the Limit* (New York: Pocket Books, 1980), 52.

5. *Insight.*

6. *Bits and Pieces,* October 1983, 24.

Chapter 9

1. Sam Shoemaker, *And Love Thy Neighbor* (Waco, Tex.: Word Books, 1967), 11–13.

2. Festo Kivengere, *I Love Idi Amin* (Old Tappan, N.J.: Fleming H. Revell, 1977), 62.

Chapter 10

1. *Los Angeles Times,* October 12, 1982.

2. *Christopher News Notes* No. 240.

DATE DUE